Biography and Political Uses of Memory

Socialist History 34

Rivers Oram Press
London, Sydney and Chicago

Editorial Board

Geoff Andrews	Nina Fishman	Kevin Morgan
Stefan Berger	David Howell	Emmet O'Connor
John Callaghan	Karen Hunt	David Parker
Andy Croft	Dianne Kirby	Willie Thompson
Allison Drew	Neville Kirk	Mike Waite
Elizabeth Fidlon	Michael Macedo	Chris Williams
Andrew Flinn	Kevin McDermott	

Editorial Advisers: Carlos Cunha, Eric Hobsbawm, Boris Kagarlitsky, Gregory Kealey, Victor Kiernan, Stuart Macintyre, David Marquand, Lungisile Ntsebeza, Donald Sassoon, John Saville, Pat Thane

Editorial Enquiries: Gidon Cohen, School of Government and International Affairs, Southend House, Durham University, Durham DH1 3TG or gidon.cohen@durham.ac.uk

Reviews Enquiries: Matthew Worley, Department of History, University of Reading, Whiteknights, Reading, RG6 6AA or m.worley@reading.ac.uk

Socialist History 34 was edited by Norman LaPorte, Stephen Hopkins, Gidon Cohen and Matthew Worley

Published in 2009
by Rivers Oram Press, an imprint of Rivers Oram Publishers Ltd
144 Hemingford Road, London, N1 1DE

Distributed in the USA by
Independent Publishers Group, Franklin Street, Chicago, IL 60610
Distributed in Australia and New Zealand by
UNIReps, University of New South Wales, Sydney, NSW 2052

Set in Garamond by NJ Design
and printed in Great Britain by T.J. International Ltd, Padstow

This edition copyright © 2009 Socialist History Society
The articles are copyright © 2009 Stephen Hopkins, Francis King, Emmet O'Connor, Reiner Tosstorff, Giuseppe Vatalaro

No part of this journal may be produced in any form, except for the quotation of brief passages in criticism, without the written permission of the publishers. The right of the contributors to be identified as the authors has been asserted by them in accordance with the Copyright, Designs and Patents Act 1988

British Library Cataloguing in Publication Data
A catalogue record for this publication is available from the British Library

ISBN 978 1 85489 171 6 (pb)
ISSN 0969 4331

Contents

Notes on Contributors — iv

Editorial — vi
Norman LaPorte
Stephen Hopkins

Alexander Lozovsky — 1
Sketch of a Bolshevik Career
Reiner Tosstorff

Vladimir Aleksandrovich Bazarov (1874–1939) — 20
One of the First Dissident Communists
Francis King

Identity and Self-Representation in Irish Communism
The Connolly Column and the Spanish Civil War — 36
Emmet O'Connor

Comparing Revolutionary Narratives — 52
Irish Republican Self-presentation and Considerations for
the study of Communist Life Histories
Stephen Hopkins

Perspectives — 70
Berlinguer's 'Democratic Alternative'
Giuseppe Vatalaro

Books to Remember — 91
Ralph Miliband, *Parliamentary Socialism*

Reviews — 95

Notes on Contributors

Stephen Hopkins is a Lecturer in the Department of Politics and International Relations at the University of Leicester. He has research interests in the field of the Northern Ireland conflict and its legacy, and the politics of autobiography and memoir. Recent publications include chapters on contemporary political memoir in Northern Ireland in Liam Harte (ed.), *Modern Irish Autobiography: Self, Nation and Society* (Palgrave Macmillan, 2007), and Mervyn Busteed, Frank Neal and Jon Tonge (eds), *Irish Protestant Identities* (Manchester University Press, 2008).

Francis King is a researcher in Russian and Soviet History, translator and interpreter. He is also treasurer of the *Socialist History Society*.

Emmet O'Connor is a senior lecturer in politics in the University of Ulster, Magee College. He is a former editor of *Saothar*, journal of the Irish Labour History Society, and author of various publications on labour history, including *Reds and the Green: Ireland, Russia, and the Communist Internationals, 1919–43* (2004), and 'Behind the legend: Waterfordmen in the International Brigades in the Spanish Civil War', *Decies: Journal of the Waterford Archaeological and Historical Society* (2005).

Reiner Tosstorff teaches history at the Johannes Gutenberg University of Mainz. He is the author of a history of the Profintern in German (Paderborn 2004). Other recent publications cover the history of the POUM in the Spanish Civil War and aspects of the history of the International Labour Organisation in the inter-war period.

Giuseppe Vatalaro has an MA in sociology from the University of Kent, Canterbury and a PhD in Italian Politics from Swansea University. He is currently working in the School of European Studies, Cardiff University and is researching the history of the Italian Communist Party.

Editorial

The diversity of biographical approaches to history that this issue of *Socialist History* has as its theme were first presented as papers at a series of one-day conferences on aspects of communism at the Universities of Manchester, Leicester and Glamorgan during 2007–8. We hope, as co-organisers of these events (together with former *Socialist History* editor, Kevin Morgan) that the articles benefited from the discussions they inspired. We hope, too, that we will be able to continue the series of communism seminars into 2009 and beyond. Readers interested in revolutionary communist trade unionism and its links with and differences from syndicalism should note that a special issue of *Anarchist Studies* in the autumn of 2009 will draw on the Glamorgan leg of the seminar series.

In the first two articles, the biographies of two mid-level Bolshevik leaders are brought into the spotlight in an undertaking made possible by the more recent opening of the archives. Alexander Lozovsky, the General Secretary of the Red International of Labour Unions (RILU), the trade-union wing of the Communist International, is the subject of Reiner Tosstorff's biographical sketch. As Tosstorff—whose recent work on the RILU makes him a foremost subject expert—observes, relatively little is known, especially to English-language readers, about the pre-revolutionary political development of one of Stalin's loyal executors. The article shows that, despite Lozovsky's own efforts to rewrite his political past, his early relationship with Bolshevism was one of conflict and rupture. Born in 1878 in the Pales of Settlement into a poor Jewish family, Lozovsky's initial politicisation at the turn of the century led him to take up underground work for the Bolsheviks. However, as a political émigré in France, the constant feuds and tensions in the movement led to him turning his back on Russian sectarianism, opting instead for an unusually high degree of integration in the French left, in particular as a trade unionist. It was only the outbreak of the war and the February Revolution that prompted his return to Russian politics. Even then, however, Lozovsky initially continued to come into serious conflict with Bolshevism's construction of the one-party state. As Tosstorff points out, Lozovsky's shifting political identity is symbolised by his changing names: as a French trade unionist he used his 'real' family name, Dridzo, but as a Bolshevik he takes on the pseudonym 'Lozovsky'.

To borrow a phrase coined by Francis King, the author of the second of these biographical sketches, Lozovsky stood 'between Menshevism and Bolshevism'—an ambiguity unwelcome during the search for 'enemies' that characterised life in the later 1920s and, above all, the 1930s. Notably, both men suffered during Stalin's later purges, despite one becoming a party-loyalist and the other—as King calls him—'one of the first dissident communists'. Born in Tula 1874, Bazarov was Lozovsky's contemporary. But their social origins differed. Bazarov was the son of a provincial doctor, who was politicised as a student on a journey leading from 'narodnic' socialism to the 'scientific method' Marxism. Notably, Bazarov was not only a leading authority on Marx, but the co-translator of Marx's most influential translation into Russian. While Lozovsky left the acrimonious infighting of the Bolsheviks behind, Bazarov—who had joined the Bolsheviks in 1904— took part in these debates, making scholarly and journalistic contributions to them. Nevertheless, both men shared the hope that the Russian Social Democratic and Labour Party could be reunited. In 1917, in an expression of this, they were both involved with Gorky's newspaper, *Novaya zhizn'*, and the 'United Social-Democrat Internationalists' that grew out of it. They also shared a disdain for the growth of the one-party state, its censorship and repression. Yet, both men's idealism led them to become officials in the new Russia. In Bazarov's case, it was a belief that the New Economic Policy (1921–8) could provide the economic foundation on which a new socialist society could emerge. Both articles provide fascinating insights into how diverse were the biographies of Soviet party and state officials, and how this diversity remained throughout most of the 1920s.

In the following two articles, Emmet O'Connor and Stephen Hopkins analyse communist self-presentation and life-histories in the context of the ambivalent interaction between communism and nationalism in Ireland in the twentieth century, both north and south. For O'Connor, the development of communism in Ireland, though hampered by the suffocating power of clericalism, was intimately bound up with the presence and strength of republican separatism. However, the relationship between the universalist goals of international communism and the narrower, and sometimes parochial, concerns of Irish nationalism, was never straightforward or simple to negotiate. Despite the apparent weakness of Irish communism as a political movement, and the dearth of self-presentation from within this small, often beleaguered community, O'Connor argues forcefully that communists did play a significant role in some of the key episodes of radical history in Ireland. In particular, memoirs and reflections on the experience of Irish communists in the 'Connolly Column' of the International Brigades have provided historians with some important resources for understanding the movement, and its central characters.

The article contends that, in the teeth of clerical support for Franco's rebellion, 'the twin pillars of opposition to Franco in the Free State were the CPI and the Republican Congress'. The latter was a 1930s left-wing offshoot of the IRA, and during the Spanish war, these organisations came to share a 'communist republicanism', comprising a belief in 'the politics of anti-imperialism at home, and the popular front internationally.' Of the handful of memoirs that exist, O'Connor recognises the effort made to compare the struggles of Spanish and Irish Republicanism; he cites Peadar O'Donnell's *Salud! An Irishman in Spain* (1937), 'I walked into a Civil War in Achill just as I walked into one in Spain, and it was the same Civil War…A picture of Achill is a map of Spain.' But, relations were sometimes strained, not least with the largely Protestant, anti-partition and yet anti-IRA members of labour organisations in Northern Ireland. O'Connor finishes his illuminating article by offering some provocative thoughts on how we should interpret the recent wave of commemoration of the 'Connolly Column' in Ireland. For many radicals and trade unionists in modern Ireland, the memory of 'Spain', from the 1980s onwards, has been corralled into service as part of the battle to defeat the Catholic hierarchy's grip on social power; 'the Connolly Column became re-imagined as a prophetic forerunner of modern, pluralist Ireland.' However, O'Connor reminds us that the bulk of Irish volunteers for the Spanish Republic identified *both* with the Comintern outlook and with a more rooted and local view of the struggle: 'They saw the war in Spain not simply as a clash of global ideologies, but as a struggle of people like themselves—small holders, farm labourers, and workers—against very familiar enemies: bishops, the army, and big landowners.'

Stephen Hopkins analyses the self-presentation of a different generation of Irish republicans, focusing on the Provisional movement of the post-1969 period and in particular the political memoirs of the Sinn Féin President, Gerry Adams. The article endeavours to draw some preliminary comparative points between the narrative of Adams, the leader of a nationalist revolutionary movement, and West European communist leaders like Harry Pollitt or Maurice Thorez. It is argued that if there has been a dearth of comparative study of the biographical dimension within the context of communist historiography, attempts to compare communism with other self-proclaimed revolutionary or radical movements are even rarer. Hopkins denies that the Provisional Republican movement can be understood in terms of a close ideological convergence with communist parties, but it has shared several similarities in terms of both structure and internal organisation. Despite a strong suspicion of electoralism, and a parallel fear of being co-opted into the existing political system, these revolutionary organisations have followed similar trajectories, involving their progressive incorporation and the 'slide' into reformism. Both Provisionals and western communists have, at different times, engaged in clandestine and conspiratorial political activity, although the former's recourse to the use of a sustained campaign of political violence is not shared by western communist parties. In terms of internal organisation, the position of power occupied by Gerry Adams in the Provisional movement (both the IRA and Sinn Féin) over the course of at least thirty years has a clear parallel in the position of various long-serving general secretaries of communist parties. However, although Adams has been a hugely popular leader, it is also the case that this power has not always been uncontested; dissident voices have been raised, particularly in recent times, complaining about the neutering of the movement's revolutionary vocation.

As with the autobiographical writing of communist leaders, Adams's political memoirs may be interpreted as an example of what Morgan has termed a 'personalised form of official party history.' Hopkins goes on to consider Adams's writing on the basis of three dimensions: anonymity, combativity and teleology. The article examines the assimilation of the author's individual voice to the collective ethos and values, the bureaucratic 'persona' of the party, and draws attention to some of the distinctive elements in Adams's emblematic account, in comparison with those of communist leaders. As far as conveying the movement's struggle is concerned, Adams has faced a particularly problematic dilemma: he has continued to deny ever having been a member, let alone a leader, of the Provisionals' military wing, the IRA. This stance has provoked the derision of critics and biographers, and the article investigates the rationale for this insistence, and the problems it has entailed. Finally, there is an effort to describe the teleological conceit at the heart of Adams's narrative, and the article concludes by positing a number of potential points of connection between the construction of exemplary Irish republican and west European communist lives.

It is to be hoped that this issue of *Socialist History* provides some food for thought for researchers interested in the biographical dimension of the study of communist history, a field that remains ripe for further exploration. Those interested in a future series of seminars devoted to aspects of communist and revolutionary history, please contact Norry LaPorte (nlaporte@glam.ac.uk) or Stephen Hopkins (sh15@le.ac.uk).

Norman LaPorte
University of Glamorgan
Stephen Hopkins
University of Leicester

Socialist History Titles

Requests for back issues to ro@riversoram.com

Previous issues of *Socialist History* include:

22 Revolutions and Revolutionaries
...John Newsinger on Irish Labour; Allison Drew on experiences of the gulag; Edward Acton, Monty Johnstone, Boris Kagarlitsky, Francis King and Hillel Ticktin on the significance of 1917...
1 85489 151 0

23 Migrants and Minorities
...Shivdeep Grewal on racial politics of the National Front, Keith Copley and Cronain O'Kelly on the British Irish in Chartist times; Stephen Hipkin on rural conflict in early modern Britain...
1 85489 155 3

24 Interesting Times?
...David Howell interviews Eric Hobsbawm; John Callaghan on reviews of *Interesting Times*; Ann Hughes on Christopher Hill's work; Cambridge communists reminisce...
1 85489 157 X

25 Old Social Movements?
...Meg Allen on women, humour and the Miners' Strike; Paul Burnham on the squatters of 1946; David Young on agency and ethnicity; Charles Hobday on the Fifth Monarchy...
1 85489 158 8

26 Youth Cultures and Politics
...Rich Palser on the Woodcraft Folk; Richard Cross on anarcho-punk; Michelle Webb on the LLY; Jonathan Grossman on apartheid...
1 85489 159 6

27 Rethinking Social Democracy
...Stefan Berger on the democracy gap; Andrew Thorpe on 'progressive' disunity; Aad Blok on Jan Tinbergen; Willie Thompson interview with Donald Sassoon...
1 85489 160 X

28 The Abyssinia Crisis
...Willie Thompson on Italian troops in Abyssinia; Christian Hogsbjerg on C.L.R. James and *The Black Jacobins*; David Howell on the 1935 general election in Britain...
1 85489 161 8

29 Collaboratiom, Resistance and the Unions
...Emmet OConnor on British unions in Ireland; Jonathan Jeffries on Gibraltar; Steve Cushion on the 1941 French Miners' Strike; Sarah Glynn on British Bengali politics...
1 85489 162 6

30 1956 and the New Left
...Lesley Hardy on E.P. Thompson and F.R. Leavis; Grant Pooke on Francis Klingender; Sebastian Berg on *New Left Review* and *Dissent*...
978 1 85489 163 1

31 Imperialism
...considers the changing nature of imperialism in the period since the Second World War...
978 1 85489 164 8

32 Activism
...lifts the lid on four different political organisations—the British Communist Party, the Labour Party, the Co-operative movement and the British Union of Fascists.
978 1 85489 169 3

33 Origins of the French Revolution
...Attacks the idea of the Revolution as bourgeois and popular with deep, long-term economic and social causes and shows its origins to be located in the intellectual and cultural discourses of the late eighteenth century
978 1 85489 170 9

Alexander Lozovsky
Sketch of a Bolshevik Career

Reiner Tosstorff

Recent interest in the biography of the Soviet official, Alexander Lozovsky, has been the result of his fate in connection with the Jewish Antifascist Committee, against which, in 1952, Stalin initiated a secret trial as a significant part of the last great, unambiguously anti-Semitic wave of 'purges'.[1] The focus on his final years, however, pushes his earlier activity into the background. That Lozovsky's was not one of the really significant Bolshevik leaders does not need to be stressed. Despite a certain worldliness, which he had acquired in exile and enabled him to become a specialist in the Soviet state on world events, he undoubtedly did not have the intellectual depth and the strength of political leadership of a Lenin, Trotsky or Bukharin, to say nothing of Stalin's unscrupulous desire for power. Even when, as General Secretary of the Red International of Labour Unions (RILU) from 1921 until 1937, he embodied the communist claim to leadership in the international trade-union movement and thereby achieved a degree of international recognition, he remained a man of the second rank, who exercised more advisory than decision-making functions. Yet, it is noteworthy that, until 1949—despite 'problematic' periods until 1920—Lozovsky continually held significant functions.

Admittedly he is mentioned throughout much of the existing literature. Yet the various transformations, which Lozovsky himself 'ironed out' after 1920, have repeatedly led to mistaken information in these individual depictions of his life. This was particularly the case when he was not at the centre of the narrative and his concrete position was not made clear from the relevant sources. Some confusion has also been caused by the usage of his names. This relates less to 'Dridzo' and 'Lozovsky' than to his forenames—the actual 'Solomon Abramovič' and the more commonly used 'Alexander'. Many historians have stumbled over the latter, which was an assumed name that became a sort of confidential party name during his years as head of the Red International of Labour Unions. In their trawl through the newly opened archives of the International, historians were unable to uncover the identity of 'Alexander'.[2] Of course, these difficulties for historians have something to do with the manner in which Lozovsky adapted his biography and identity to changing demands. A particular example of this is his entry in the biographies and autobiographies of the new Bolshevik élite, which was published in the mid-1920s in the *Encyclopaedia Granat*.[3] In a French edition, which limits itself to the most important individuals—whose entries have been extended—the editors, Georges Haupt and Jean-Jacques Marie, use Lozovsky as an example in their detailed introduction on the problems of this construction of identity:

> The biographies of those who wavered between one side and the other before and after 1917 are characterised by discretion concerning the political aspects of their lives as militants. Men like Lozovsky say little or nothing about their political changes.[4]

The following biographical sketch limits itself to the significant stages of his life until the year 1920 when, after many twists and turns, he finally joined the Bolshevik Party and took on, at a more subordinate level, trade-union function in the new Soviet Republic. The following year, a combination of particular, in a certain sense coincidental, circumstances then catapulted him into a leadership role in the international communist movement. From 1921 until 1937, during its entire existence, he was the unrivalled leader of the RILU, the trade-union arm of the Comintern.

From the Shtetl to the Party: Socialisation between Judaism and Revolutionary Politics

Lozovsky was born on 16 [28] March 1878 as Solomon Abramovič Dridzo—to use the Russian formulation of his names—into a poor family in a village in the Alexandrovsk district of the province of Ekaterinoslav (since 1926, Dnepropetrovsk)—in other words, in the Pale of Settlement.[5] His unusual family name, which was certainly not typical for Jews in the Russian Empire, is explained by his Sephardic family's resettlement after being expelled from Spain in 1492.[6] He grew up in the traditional *milieu* of the Shtetl. His father was a teacher at cheder, the Jewish school. His mother, who was illiterate, had a market stall. The family had, in total, seven children. Their mother tongue was Yiddish. His father also taught him Russian, which soon after leaving the Shtetl he mastered perfectly, although he never lost his Yiddish accent.[7] Undoubtedly this cultural background helped foster his talent at learning languages. During his exile in France, he became fluent in French. In the summer of 1920, when he visited Germany with a Russian trade-union delegation, he learned German so quickly—if also in part due to the advantage of his native tongue's linguistic proximity—that the translator assigned to him by the German Communist Party stated that, 'he was pushing me out of a job'.[8]

Yet despite his eagerness to learn, which was undoubtedly already evident during his youth, the poverty of his family allowed him only autodidactic endeavours. At the age of 11, he began to work in a butcher's shop, then he was a trader at the market until he turned 14 years of age and began a three-year apprenticeship as a blacksmith, working afterwards for three years in this job. Then, however, he received the material support of a brother, who had obviously come into some wealth—about whom we know nothing—which offered social ascent through education. He began to prepare for an academic school education but, in 1899 had to complete his military service in Kazan. After this, in 1901, he passed the school-leaving certificate. At the same time, he had begun to read social-democratic literature and taken up his first political contacts. He was now on the path to becoming a professional revolutionary. After returning home for a short while, in 1903 he went to study in St Petersburg, where he was arrested for the first time at the end of October and exiled to Kazan. There he formally joined the Bolshevik faction and became a member of its local committee. The time of the Revolution of 1905 and the accompanying struggles, saw him in many places, including St Petersburg and Kharkov. He was also a delegate to the Bolshevik party conference of December 1905 in Tammerfors, where he came in direct contact with the Bolshevik leadership for the first time. Nadežda Krupskaja mentioned him as one of those whose 'reports from the localities had been so enthrallingly interesting'.[9] At the conference, he did not use the assumed name 'Alexei', which he had continued to use in Kazan. Instead, for the first time, he used the pseudonym 'Lozovsky', which was obviously taken from the name of the Losovoja railway station near his place of birth. After many more years of underground activity in various places, in the course of which he repeatedly eluded the police, he was finally arrested in 1908 and exiled to Siberia. Yet, he managed to escape and went into exile.

In France: Between Exile, Integration and Anti-War Opposition

After a sojourn in Geneva, Lozovsky reached Paris at the beginning of 1909, where one of his brothers already lived.[10] Now in a centre of Russian exiles, he lived the life of a revolutionary refugee for a lengthy period. He subsequently recalled that:

> In Paris I was secretary of the labour exchange for Russian emigrants and, for some time, headed an adult education school for electrical fitters. For two years, I was General Secretary of the hatters' trade union. I headed a backers' co-operative for ten months and, for several months, was a manager of a garage. In Paris, I completed a course at a school for taxi drivers and worked in a factory as a blacksmith and a turner.[11]

Hidden behind this laconic enumeration of various jobs are his changing political associations which, in the construction of his autobiography in the mid-1920s, he obviously wanted to render insignificant. Initially, Lozovsky was integrated into the Bolshevik group in Paris and wrote some articles for the party press. After 1908, the Conciliator tendency was formed within the Bolsheviks, whose plea for reunion of the party with the Mensheviks led to clashes with Lenin. Lozovsky belonged to them too.[12] Their most important members, Nogin and Rykov, were soon arrested while carrying out party work in Russia. According to Bertram Wolfe, '[I]t left the "Conciliator" Bolsheviks under such inept, second-string leaders as Lozovsky....He soon became sick of the squabbling and weary of the effort of opposing the implacably tireless Lenin. He gave up the struggle, concerning himself entirely with activity in the French trade-union movement'.[13] Lozovsky was not only a member of the French Socialist Party; his main activity was trade-union work with the Parisian cap-makers' section of the Federation of Hatters within the General Confederation of Labour (CGT). This French trade-union association united various political tendencies, not least of which was, of course, the Socialists. But it was dominated by revolutionary syndicalism, which formed the majority tendency and, thereby, determined policy. For Lozovsky, this too must have represented a certain break with his political past, even if he never went as far as adapting himself to the libertarian and anarchist undertones which always resonated with syndicalism. But it allowed him to become acquainted with syndicalist ideas, which proved to be to his advantage after 1921. In 1910, Lozovsky came to the attention of the cap-makers at a trade-union event through his resolute stance.[14] Founded in 1896, the trade union had been little able to assert itself within its branch of the profession. A significant characteristic was that its membership was almost completely composed of Jewish immigrants, who also made up practically all the workforce. The trade union looked for a new secretary to overcome its internal conflicts, which arose out of disputes between older members and new recruits, who had come to France after the revolution of 1905 and were more radically inclined. Lozovsky took on these tasks. Though effective trade-union work, he succeeded in increasing the organisation's membership. According to his own details, of 1,500 workers in 1912 half of them were organised. Boycotts were used highly effectively, for example, in order to have dismissals reversed. Above all, under his leadership in 1912 a pay agreement was enforced throughout the entire profession after a general strike. The trade union was able to prevent the employment of workers who were not union organised, just as it was also able to prevent a firm from strike breaking. Furthermore, he resolutely applied himself to achieving the same pay for men and women who were doing the same work.

The trade union also succeeded in expanding its welfare provision. In addition to a strike fund it now also had a fund for unemployment benefits. For the entire Jewish workers' movement in Paris an insurance scheme was set up on the model of the *Arbeiter-Ring* [Workers-Circle] that the Jewish Bund had already established in New York and London. Lozovsky was actively involved in this. Yet, that he had not become a 'mere trade unionist' is revealed in his warning in the trade-union press of the limitations that must be seen in such a practice. Admittedly it was an important means of solidarity. But the problems of unemployment and such like would be caused by capitalism, which must be overthrown in its entirety.

These two years of activity, which he ended 'for personal reasons'—of which we, as yet, know no more about—was only part of his trade-union activism. It was embedded in his role in the formation of an 'inter-trade union' committee for all Jewish workers the *Intersektsionen Byuro* in 1911. In addition to the cap-makers, it comprised other small Yiddish-speaking groups (including the bakers and tailors) and tried to represent the general interests of Jewish workers, including within the framework of the CGT. Under Lozovsky's leadership, the newspaper '*Der idischer arbayter*' was published, which appeared until the outbreak of the world war.[15] It offered information about the various professional groups and, thereby, articulated class interests against the paternalism of Jewish employers. Yet, as the newspaper's historian notes, 'the movement also reinforced the community from which it evolved'.[16] Through the raising of the cultural level, the 'immigrant worker, so often reduced to silence by the language barrier [... was to] regain his or her voice'.[17] Correspondingly, progressive Jewish literature was popularised, Yiddish-language theatre and other cultural activities supported, which again strengthened a separate group identity from that of the French workforce.

Lozovsky understood how to articulate the particular interests of Jewish (and of the other) immigrant workers *vis-à-vis* the wider movement. As a delegate at the 1912 CGT Congress, he participated in the discussion on the proposed state pension scheme in order to defend the right of foreign workers, who, according to the law, would have to pay into it, but then subsequently, would receive nothing in return.[18] In this way he also showed how much he was now influenced by the dominant ideas of syndicalism, as he joined numerous other delegates in the demand that pensions should be paid by the employers, not the state; thus following the 'analysis of a strict class war and not of a struggle against the state corresponding to the strong libertarian traditions in the trade unions'.[19]

In this way Lozovsky became an activist of the French left. Other Russian immigrants, who at least tried to come closer to the French workers' movement, did not succeed in overcoming the barriers between the 'milieux'. This was stated explicitly by Krupskaya, who notably referred to his ability to integrate while conceding that her own efforts fell short of this.[20] But she also had to acknowledge that many of the Russian political émigrés showed no great interest in agitation among immigrant workers.[21] This, however, did not mean that there were no more Bolsheviks who, in one way or another, became 'Frenchified'. More than a few were forced to work for their living in French factories (like Alexander Shliapnikov). Others found French partners. Yet the situation for Lozovsky was the 'most exceptional' insofar as it was a conscious decision to turn away from the feuds of the Russian emigrants. 'Lozovsky was one of the few Russian-Jewish Social-Democrats to bridge the Seine. Living among the Russian political refugee colony on the Left Bank, Lozovsky was also at home among the Yiddish-speaking immigrants in the Marais'.[22]

On the eve of the First World War he no longer had organisational relations with his 'national movement'. He had become Dridzo again, as the French Syndicalists knew him.[23] This return to the use of his family name can hardly be explained other than that he regarded his 'Russian commitment' as completely over and wanted to leave it behind him. Characteristically, Lozovsky 'rewrote' these years in his autobiographical entry in the *Encyclopaedia Granat* and did not mention his clear turn away from the Bolshevik Party. His integration into the French workers' movement as an alternative to the politics of the émigrés was, at best, hinted at. He also avoided mention of the specifically Jewish character of the cap-makers trade union, his role in the union's '*Intersektion Byuro*' and the newspaper, *Der idisher arbayter*. It was the outbreak of war that forced the break in his assimilation and brought him back into contact with the Russian émigré milieu—which, however, had re-grouped owing to the new requirements brought about by the war. Lozovsky himself vividly described his work in the following three years in an article for the theoretical journal of the French Communist Party (PCF) in 1924.[24] According to this, the outbreak of war (and the expected German attack on Paris) forced him, initially, to go south for six weeks. He worked on-the-side in the grape harvest near Montpellier until at the end of September he came across a copy of the newly founded Russian daily newspaper, *Golos*. Founded on the initiative of the then Menshevik, Antonov-Ovseenko, and produced under the most basic and financially poorest conditions, this newspaper became the organ of the internationalist wing of Russian Social Democracy (insofar as this was not Bolshevik, which had its own, separate newspaper).[25] Until January 1915, the newspaper was called *Golos* or *Naš Golos*; then, from September 1916, *Naše Slovo*, best known in the history of the anti-war left; and, finally, for a few months, *Načalo*. Names like Martov, who admittedly very soon left again, Trotsky, Pokrovsky, Ryazanov, Lunacharsky and Chicherin—to name only a few editors and correspondents—showed that it was a gathering point for the intellectual elite of Russian Marxism. Despite the different groupings that they represented, with few exceptions the route they took back to Russia led into the leadership of the Bolshevik Party.

Lozovsky immediately joined this circle and belonged to the permanent editors of the newspaper. At the same time, he was one of those—whose most prominent representative was Trotsky—who looked for contacts on the French anti-war left among Socialists, but above all among the CGT in the form of the revolutionary-syndicalist minority. They regularly took part in the weekly discussions in the editorial rooms of the journal *La Vie ouvrière*, which—suspended during the war—was the most significant theoretical organ of syndicalism before 1914. In 1915–6, it spawned the Committee for the Resumption of International Relations (*Comité pour la Reprise des Rélations internationales*), which was the most important germ cell of French communism. In this way, Lozovsky also established direct relations to many of those who were later to play an outstanding role in the RILU and its French section, the CGTU, such as Alfred Rosmer, Pierre Monatte and Gaston Monmousseau, to name only the most important of them.

Lozovsky's activities were not confined to internal discussions. Above all, in a continuation of his pre-war activities, he appeared at public meetings, which were mainly within the framework offered by the party. But the objectives of *Naše Slovo* in co-operating with *La Vie ouvrière* extended beyond France or the Russian exiles. Here we have an important force in driving forward the formation of an international left, which crystallised out of the conferences at Zimmerwald and Kienthal. In this French-Russian circle, Lozovsky stood on the moderate ('centrist') wing. Trotsky, for example, demanded that they break with the 'social chauvinists' and criticised the pacifist minority in the Socialist Party around Jean Longuet because, in practice, they supported the party majority's participation in waging the war. Lozovsky, by contrast, put forward a policy of influencing the minority in order to force them to the left.[26] Lozovsky himself subsequently avoided all mention of these feuds, whether in his autobiographical article for the PCF journal in 1924 or his entry in the Encyclopaedia Granat. Yet, at around the same time they were documented in the publication of Trotsky's writings from the First World War.[27]

The various political positions were illuminated in an anecdote told years later by another French member of this grouping, Marcel Martinet. One evening, when after a long meeting the Russians and French wanted to go home, they noticed that it was raining. Lozovsky (or, rather, Dridzo, as he used his 'real' name) grumbled: 'Damn! And I don't have an umbrella.' The remark was neither sensational nor worthy of reproach, but it was neither an accusation nor an urge for criticism which Trotsky wanted to formulate, just humorous and a bit playful, when he made a jolly quip that was only meant to be funny: neither a criticism nor was it asking for the criticism that Trotsky thought up and dished out: 'Comrade Dridzo, he who is afraid to go out in the rain is not likely to make a revolution.'[28]

After February 1917, Lozovsky was in no doubt that, in view of the impending radical revolution, he should return to his own country, ending his integration in France, insofar as this would have ever been possible with the limitations imposed by the French government. Immediately after the outbreak of the revolution, he had spoken at a mass rally, which was enthused by events in Russia, held at Trade-Union headquarters in Paris; among the other speakers were the metal workers' leader, Merrheim, Antonov-Ovseenko, and Charles Rappoport, who had long since been integrated into the French workers' movement.[29] The French government realised that these people were not allies in the cause of maintaining the new Russian 'revolutionary democracy's' participation in the war and, initially, acted to prevent their return home via England and Scandinavia. To change this position, it required resolute protests from Russia and also the methods employed by Lozovsky. He knew that the French government liked 'revolutionary machinations' in their own country even less than abroad, so he began to agitate systematically for the Russian revolution and against the war at party and trade-union meetings. As he recalled, 'My "harmful" propaganda got me out of this situation, [as] the French government chose the lesser of two evils and decided to let me go'.[30] In May he was finally able to set out for Russia and arrived two weeks later in England, where he came in contact with the British Socialist Party; then, travelling through Norway, Sweden and Finland, he arrived in Petrograd in June.[31]

In Russia
For the Russian Revolution, but Opposition to the Bolsheviks!

While still in Paris, Lozovsky had already begun to write for Gorky's newspaper, *Novaja žisn*. It supported the deepening of the revolution, but also criticised the Bolshevik strategy, especially after the seizure of power (and was then banned in July 1918). In a loose relationship with the newspaper, in the summer of 1917 the group of the 'United Social Democrats' was formed, after the failure to unite the Menshevik Party on an 'internationalist' platform. Apart from the second half of 1917, Lozovsky belonged to this tendency.[32]

Much more important for him, he arrived shortly before the Russian trade-union conference and, already enjoying a reputation as an experienced trade unionist, immediately took on a leading position in the trade-union movement. The February Revolution had also made possible a tremendous trade-union upswing. For the first time unions were completely legal.[33] For months after the fall of the Tsar, the trade unions—with around 1.5 million members—organised some 40 per cent of the industrial workforce.[34] At this time, the 'Third Russian Trade-Union Conference' met in Petrograd.[35] The term 'conference' (instead of 'congress' (expressed its still provisional character, even if, for the first time, a nationwide executive was elected) the All-Russian Central Council of Trade Unions. Among its important tasks was the convention of a congress as soon as this was possible.

At the conference, two groups opposed each other: On the one side was the Menshevik-led 'Group of the Representatives of Trade-Union Unity', which supported the Provisional Government and, especially, the socialist ministers in it; this meant that they also took a position in support of continuing the war. On the other side was the 'Group of Internationalists' around the Bolsheviks, whose party faction was led by the old party cadres, Pavel Milyutin and Grigori Zinoviev. But to their ranks also belonged the then 'unaligned' Socialists including David Ryazanov and Lozovsky, as well as Left Social Revolutionaries and the syndicalists. In the following weeks these 'unaligned' individuals joined the Bolsheviks. Lozovsky, as their spokesman made a total of five interventions in the discussions: in the debate of general principals, the tasks of trade unions and organisational structure and, in particular, on the issue of 'trade unions and economic struggle'. Interestingly, he did not present a position on the international question.[36] Lozovsky, as a representative of the Left, became Secretary of the new trade-union leadership. The construction of a central trade-union organisation, however, made little progress before the First Trade-Union Congress met at the beginning of 1918. The reasons for this lay in the radicalisation during the second half of 1917, the October coup and the first steps of Soviet power. That anything at all was achieved was, to a significant extent, thanks to Lozovsky. In the words of a Menshevik delegate at the first Congress, he was the 'only active' official.[37]

Lozovsky's activities in these months were determined by his trade-union work. But, at the same time, he had also arrived at a political decision: after the Third Trade-Union Conference, he joined the Bolshevik party. Little is known about his position in the internal party debates during the months between his return to the Bolsheviks and the October coup. Admittedly, as Secretary of the All-Russian Central Council of Trade Unions, he occupied a prominent position in the Russian workers' movement. But he did not belong to the party's leading circle. He did not take part in the Sixth Bolshevik Congress in August, although the role of the trade unions was an important point in the agenda.[38] Consequently, he was not a member of the Central Committee elected by the Congress. He was one of those showing greater caution, even if, in general, he went along with the Bolshevik's radical course of taking power through the Soviets.

His opposition to the party majority came to the fore after the October coup, when the question concerned the concrete form of the new power. In the intense political debates surrounding the question of building a socialist coalition government or governing alone and, more widely, the first dictatorial measures of the new power, Lozovsky took his place among the critics of Lenin and Trotsky, who were initially led by Zinoviev and Kamenev, and to whom his colleague in the trade-union leadership, Ryazanov, also belonged. In the first days of November there were resignations from the Bolshevik Central Committee and the new Council of People's Commissars. Lozovsky, who was not a member of this second body either, supported the opposition in a long letter to the Bolshevik faction in the Central Executive Committee, which was published in *Novaja žisn'* on 4 [17] November. He condemned the political line of the majority as having nothing in common with revolutionary Marxism, and announced that, in consequence, he would take a public stance on these issues. On the same day, in the Central Executive Committee—on which he sat together with Ryazanov as a trade-union representative—he voted with the 'right'

Bolsheviks and Left Social Revolutionaries against censoring the bourgeois press. Throughout the entire day, he participated in discussions about forming a socialist coalition government, which had been initiated by the railway workers' union (Vikzel).[39] What differentiated Lozovsky from the other oppositional Bolsheviks was that, after a few days or weeks, he did not lower his expectations and again submitted to party discipline. No one went as far as he did in proclaiming an open struggle against the Bolshevik leadership. As a result, in the trade-union newspaper *Professional'nyj vestnik*, he took the following stance:

> The tasks of the trade unions and of the Soviet power are the isolation of the bourgeois elements, who led strikes and sabotage, but this isolation should not be achieved merely by mechanical means, by arrests, by shipping to the front or by deprivation of bread cards. Preliminary censorship, the destruction of newspapers, the annihilation of freedom of agitation for the socialist and democratic parties is for us absolutely inadmissible. The closing of the newspapers, violence against strikers, etc., irritated open wounds. There has been too much of this type of 'action' recently in the memory of the Russian toiling masses and this can lead to an analogy deadly to the Sovier power.[40]

That he voted against the dissolution of the Constituent Assembly in the Central Executive Committee on 6 [19] January 1918 was logical and derived from his support for a socialist coalition government.[41]

Finally, what underlay his opposition to the Bolshevik dictatorship was a completely different estimation of the country's social situation and, thus, of the tasks of the revolution.[42] Admittedly, he too was of the opinion that the Provisional Government had failed and the country's most pressing problems could only by solved by the Soviets. But, at the same time, he believed that Russia was not ready for socialism—a view based on traditional Marxism as embodied in the Menshevik's 'orthodoxy'. Consequently, the leadership of the economy should not be taken on; rather, they should only introduce 'workers' control'. Admittedly, Lenin had issued such a decree as one of the first measures of Soviet power. In the discussion on this in the Central Executive Committee, Lozovsky played an important role.[43] For him, it was not least to stem the 'syndicalism' of the factory committees which, step by step, took over the individual factories without embedding them in the central economic administration. In this way, the central Soviet authorities as well as the trade unions were forced to the fringes. Lozovsky defended his position in a pamphlet published in the first days of 1918.

In it, he detailed how the country was not ready for the introduction of socialism; it was not a question of the country's economic organisation, but, instead, the regulation of production.[44] Accordingly, he also opposed the increasing socialisation of the economy, such as the nationalisation of the banking sector at the end of 1917.[45] For him, his ideas centred on the defence of the workforce's economic interests by the trade unions. In this way, he obviously underestimated the collapse of the entire economy and the *de facto* boycott by the employers, and entertained the illusion of being able to control a broad, spontaneous movement in the factories from above. Immediately after the publication of his letter in *Novaja žisn'*, he was expelled from the party by the Central Committee. However, as 'some comrades' thought this was a temporary measure, it was not published (and not put into effect).[46] At the end of December, he was finally expelled because, as it was stated in the resolution, his views contradicted those of the party and represented a petty-bourgeois rejection of the dictatorship of the proletariat.[47] It occurred only a few days before the first Russian Trade-Union Congress, which met from 7–14 [20–27] January 1918.[48] This, too, took place against the background of the Bolshevik seizure of power. It was characterised by repeated violent clashes and numerous interjections giving cause for breaks in the proceedings. While it was in session, the Constituent Assembly was dissolved. As a consequence, the trade unions became institutions of the new state, whose tasks now involved supporting the government; hence, we can speak of their 'state-ification' (to adopt Brügmann's translation of *ogosudarstvlenije*). The Mensheviks opposed this, demanding instead their independence (*nezavisimost*) from any subordination to party and state. Lozovsky, despite vehement opposition to the Bolsheviks after his expulsion from the party—represented an intermediate position as in all of his declarations of belief in the class war and the soviets he put forward his own concept of 'self-reliance' (*samostojatel'nost'*).[49] The Bolsheviks, despite the majority they achieved, were unable to appoint a new, stable trade-union leadership; it was not until some months later that an actual leadership group was formed around Mikhail Tomsky. Lozovsky now lost his central position in the trade-union leadership.

Until June 1918, Lozovsky remained Secretary of the Central Council of Trade Unions, but was now 'immured' by an overwhelming Bolshevik majority. From May until June of the same year, he was also Secretary of the textile workers' union; then, from June 1918 until March 1919, Secretary of the railway workers' union. In January 1919, as a representative of the non-Bolshevik trade unionists to the Second Trade-Union Congress, he repeated his criticisms concerning the necessity of trade-union independence in the most resolute of terms—yet continued to distance himself from the fundamental opposition of the Mensheviks.[50] He was elected onto the All-Russian Council of Trade Unions. In March 1919, he took over the organisation and instruction department in the All-Russian Council of Trade Unions, and became editor of its new central organ, *Professional'noe dviženie*. This was obviously an expression of his gradual rapprochement with the victors in the civil war, in which he played no military role.[51] In the meantime, he had founded a political home in the grouping of 'Social Democrat Internationalist' which, at the beginning of 1918, grew out the Social Democratic Russian Workers' Party splinter group, the 'United Social Democrats', which stood between the Bolsheviks and Mensheviks, and was grouped around *Novaja žisn'*.[52] Since early 1918, Lozovsky was a member of the group's leadership and headed their central organ, *Proletarij*. Not only did he represent them in the trade unions; he spent most of his time representing them in the Central Executive Committee, where he played the role of spokesman of the legal and ultimately loyal opposition.[53] To the extent that the Bolsheviks prevailed, he took up a new position as expressed in a pamphlet distributed by the railway workers' union in 1919. He professed support for the October Revolution, which had opened the way for the construction of socialism. But he still did not say a single word about the leading role of the Bolshevik Party. Instead, he spoke of the leading role of the trade unions in the economy.[54] His rapprochement with the Bolsheviks now took place very quickly. Already in March 1919, in a message of greetings to the Congress of the Russian Communist Party, he stated that, in the fire of revolution, there were practically no more differences of opinion. In his party, the only topic of discussion now was how to create unity.[55] In December 1919, the fourth congress of the Russian Socialist Workers' Party—as it called itself after several split-offs and fusions leaving only 422 members—voted to join the Bolsheviks. The Bolshevik Party accepted them on an individual basis, while recognising their previous membership.[56]

Towards a New Task: Organising the International Trade-Union Movement for Communism [57]

Finally he had become Lozovsky. Characteristically, it was now this name that he exclusively used, leaving 'Dridzo' behind in his French past. As a consequence of his reconciliation with the Bolsheviks, he found his way back to climbing the career ladder as a professional trade-union leader. In 1920, he became chairman of the Moscow district's trade-union council. In the trade-union debate that shook the Bolshevik Party in the winter of

1920–1, he was one of the 'Platform of Ten', which was led by Lenin and Zinoviev and finally enforced its position in the Party. But he did not yet receive a leading position in the Party. (It was only under Stalin that he was promoted to the Central Committee, and even then he could not be viewed as an actual Party leader.) Instead, in the summer of 1920, he was assigned as a guide for accompanying foreign trade unionists visiting the new Russia. Out of this assignment grew a new role, in a manner more 'organic' than planned. He was one of the few Bolsheviks with international trade-union experience. Thanks to his time in France he was familiar with, in particular, revolutionary syndicalism and, furthermore, he spoke several languages. Now his role was to proselytise those foreign activists, who had not only an abstract interest in the Russian experience but were also interested in establishing direct organisational connections. It was in this rather chance manner that the RILU was founded as an alternative to the Social Democratic-led trade-union international, the International Federations of Trade Unions (IFTU), but also to the syndicalists's efforts for a revolutionary trade-union international politically and organisationally independent from the Bolsheviks. Lozovsky took the leading role in the first discussions about this in the summer of 1920 and then prepared its foundation in July 1921. Tomsky, the Bolshevik's trade-union chairman, had little time for these activities on account of his many other commitments, not least of which was as a member of the Politburo. When, in May 1921, Tomsky was transferred for disciplinary reasons to Turkestan for six months—he had taken a 'false position' in the trade-union debate—the position of General Secretary of the new trade-union international fell, more or less automatically, to Lozovsky. The Politburo's short-lived idea of appointing Jan Rudzutak proved to be impractical. He was completely unknown in the western European trade-union movement and, thus, his appointment came up against opposition.

Lozovsky's biography was now intertwined with the history of the RILU during the sixteen years of its existence. For the international communist movement, it was unique that he survived the drastic political and organisational turns of the following period always remaining in the same leadership. This was only possible because he proved himself to be a loyal Stalinist, despite—perhaps even because of—his biography with its multifarious ruptures. Of course, it is also important that the RILU was not at the centre of the communist movement. All said and done, his position was of subordinate significance. However, we should stress that the defence and maintenance of its existence against various attempts to put this in question was always his main concern. This was especially evident in the mid-1920s, when its dissolution was a topical issue following the formation of the Anglo-Russian Trade-Union Committee. When there was an opportunity to create a greater role for the RILU, such as after 1929 during the ultra-left policy with the formation globally of 'revolutionary trade unions', he was an enthusiastic protagonist of the new course. However, in 1936–7 he had to experience the winding down of the RILU, without being able to actively oppose this in any way. It was in this manner that he lost his own 'institutional' and 'international' basis and became a Soviet official. His posts included that of a professor of history and, after 1939, he served as deputy foreign minister under Molotov. Despite his past, with its many 'dubious' aspects, he survived the Great Terror of 1937; indeed, he was one of the few elected to the Central Committee in 1934 to remain in their position. During the Second World War, his international experience was again useful to Stalin, who appointed him to head the Soviet Information Bureau and to act as party overseer in the Jewish Antifascist Committee. This last position, however, sealed his fate when Stalin initiated his last great wave of purges.

Acknowledgements
This chapter was translated by Norman LaPorte.

Notes

1. See, for example, Shimon Redlich (ed.), *War, Holocaust and Stalinism: a documented study of the Jewish Antifascist Committee in the USSR* (Luxembourg, 1995); Joshua Rubinstein and Vladimir P. Naumov (eds), *Stalin's Secret Pogrom. The Postwar Inquisition of the Jewish Anti-Fascist Committee* (London, 2002).
2. See, for example, Frederic Wakeman, *Policing Shanghai: 1927–1937* (Berkeley, 1996), p.148; Harvey Klehr, John Earl Haynes and Fridrikh Igorevich Firsov (eds), *The Secret World of American Communism* (New Haven and London, 1995), pp.54, 61.
3. See the reprint of the Encyclopaedia, *Dejateli SSSR i revoljucionnogo dviženija Rossii. Enciklopedičeskij slovar' Granat* (Moscow, 1989), pp.513–15 (Lozovsky).
4. For the English translation, see Georges Haupt and Jean-Jacques Marie (eds), *Makers of the Russian Revolution. Biographies of Bolshevik Leaders* (London, 1974), p.210.
5. These biographical details about his youth have been largely taken from his autobiographical entry in the *Encyclopaedia Granat*. During his time at the RILU, he normally used the name A. Lozovsky (i.e. Alexander), above all in his numerous publications. Here, his own usage is followed.
6. These otherwise unknown details were given by Lozovsky during the trial of 1952. See, Rubinstein and Naumov, *Stalin's Secret Pogrom*, p.221.

7. This, according to one former KPD leader who was also a Russian Jew, sounded 'terrible'. This may have contributed to him being known to his collaborators inRILU by his nickname "Rebbe' (Rabbi). See, Arkadij Maslow, 'Losowski— Schmied, Volkskommissar, 'Rebbe" [11. Juli 1941]', in Ruth Fischer and Arkadij Maslow, *Abtrünnig wider Willen. Aus Briefen und Manuskripten des Exils* (edited by Peter Lübbe), Munich, 1990, (408 412), p. 409.
8. Rosa Leviné-Meyer, *Inside German Communism. Memories of Party Life in the Weimar Republic* (London, 1977), p.13.
9. Nadezhda Krupskaya, *Memories of Lenin* (London, 1970), p.128.
10. Olivia Gomolinski, 'Un modèle de mediation culturelle et politique: la période parisienne de Solomon Abramovitch Dridzo, dit Alexandre Lozovsky (1909– 1917)', *Archives Juives*, 2 (2001), p.20.
11. *Dejateli SSSR*, p.514.
12. On the Conciliators, see Leonard Schapiro, *The Communist Party of the Soviet Union* (London, 1960), pp.115–24, 126ff; Robert V. Daniels, *The Conscience of Revolution. Communist Opposition in Soviet Russia* (Cambridge MA, 1960), pp.26–8.
13. Bertram D. Wolfe, *Three Who Made a Revolution. A Biographical History* (New York, 1948), p.527ff. This negative characterisation of Lozovsky is, however, certainly determined by the author's experience in the 1920s as the leader of a faction in the CPUSA, which found themselves in constant feuds with him on questions of communist trade-union policy. See his autobiography, Wolfe, *A Life in Two Centuries. An Autobiography* (New York, 1981), in which there are several similar statements.
14. The following discussion is based on, Nancy L. Green, *The Pletzl of Paris. Jewish Immigrant Workers in the Belle Epoque* (New York and London, 1986), pp.155–71; see also Paula Hyman, *From Dreyfus to Vichy. The Remaking of French Jewry, 1906–1939* (New York, 1979), pp.92–9; Gomolinski, Un modèle.
15. See Green, 'Der idisher arbayter', in Christiane Herwig and Dirk Hoerder (eds), *The Press of Labor Migrants in Europe and North America 1880s to 1930s* (Bremen, 1985), pp.89–111. For an overview of the entire Jewish trade-union spectrum in Paris, see Green, *Pletzl of Paris*, pp.149–155.
16. Green, 'Der idisher arbayter', p.102.
17. Green, 'Der idisher arbayter', p.103.
18. *XVIIIe Congrès national corporatif (XIIe de la CGT) et 5ème conférence des Bourses du Travail. Tenus au Havre du 16 au 23 septembre 1912. Compte rendu sténographique* (Le Havre, undated), p.167. Lozovsky began his short intervention by apologising for his poor French.
19. Gomolinski, 'Un modèle', p.23. More generally, see Bruno Dumons and Gilles Pollet, "Une contre-société ouvrière en lutte: La CGT et le debat sur les retraites fin XIXe—début XXe siècle", *Revue d'histoire moderne et contemporaine*, 2 (1997), pp.228–51.
20. Krupskaya, *Memories*, p.181.
21. This was particularly the case among women, see Krupskaya, *Memories*, p.196.
22. Green, *Pletzl of Paris*, p.157.
23. See, for example, Colette Chambelland and Jean Maitron (eds), *Syndicalisme*

révolutionnaire et communisme. Les archives de Pierre Monatte 1914–1926 (Paris 1968), *passim*.
24. A. Lozovsky, 'Comment nous éditions pendant la guerre des journaux internationalistes', *Bulletin communiste*, Nr 41, 21.10.1924, pp.1020–3, Nr 42, 31.10.1924, pp.1040–2.
25. On this newspaper and the group associated with it, see the autobiographically informed comments of Alfred Rosmer, idem., *Le mouvement ouvrier pendant la guerre. Bd.1. De l'union sacrée à Zimmerwald* (Aubervilliers, 1993), pp.244–9; see also, Harvey Goldberg, Georges Haupt, and Marc Lagana (eds), *Une vie révolutionnaire 1883–1940. Les mémoires de Charles Rappoport* (Paris, 1991), pp.316–26; for extensive details, see Michael E. Shaw, 'The Nashe Slovo group and Russian Social Democracy during World War I: the search for unity' (PhD thesis: University of Indiana, 1975). On the significance of this for the formation of a French anti-war left, see also the standard works on the revolutionary French left at this time, Annie Kriegel, *Aux origines du communisme français* (2 vols: Den Haag and Paris, 1964) und Robert Wohl, *French Communism in the Making, 1914–1924* (Stanford, 1966).
26. See, for example, Wohl, *French Communism*, p.77. See, also, the comments in Pierre Broué, *Trotsky* (Paris, 1988), p.149. Insight into the various positions inside *Naše Slovo* are provided in the documentation by A. E. Senn, 'The Politics of Golos and *Nashe Slovo*, *International Review of Social History*, 3 (1972), pp. 675–704.
27. In the French edition, see Léon Trotsky, *La guerre et la révolution. Le naufrage de la IIe Internationale, les débuts de la IIIe Internationale* (Paris 1974), vol.2, pp.154ff.
28. Marcel Martinet, 'Quelques souvenirs' [1934], *Cahiers Léon Trotsky*, 12 (November 1982), p.12.
29. Goldberg et. al. (eds), *Une vie révolutionnaire*, p.351.
30. Lozovsky, 'Comment nous éditions', p.1042.
31. Walter Kendall, *The Revolutionary Movement in Britain 1900–1921. The Origins of British Bolshevism* (London, 1969), pp.171ff., 377.
32. See, Francis King, 'Between Bolshevism and Menshevism: The Social-Democratic Internationalists in the Russian Revolution', *Revolutionary Russia*, 1 (1996), pp.1–18.
33. On the trade unions during the revolution, see Uwe Brügmann, *Die russischen Gewerkschaften in Revolution und Bürgerkrieg 1917–1919* (Frankfurt, 1972); Gennady Shkliarevsky, *Labor in the Russian Revolution. Factory Committees and Trade Unions, 1917–1918* (New York, 1993).
34. Shkliarevsky, *Labor*, p.66.
35. On the convening and course of the conference, see Shkliarevsky, *Labor*, pp.68, 72–9; Brügmann, Die russischen Gewerkschaften, pp.58–77. The protocol was not published for a further ten years. Its publication by the Historical Institute of the Soviet Trade Unions, ISTPROF came with an extensive introduction by the director of the institution, see Jurij Milonov (ed.) *Tret'ja vserossijskaja konferencija professional'nych sojuzov 3–11 ijulja (20–28 ijunja st. st.) 1917. Stenograficeskij otcet* (Moscow, 1927).

36. *Tret'ja vserossijskaja konferencija*, pp.98ff, 255–7, 283ff, 344ff, 349ff.
37. *Pervyj vserossijskij s-ezd professional'nych sojuzov. 7–14 janvarja 1918g. Pol'nyj stenograficeskij otcet s predisloviem M. Tomskogo* (Moscow, 1918), p.52. See also, the introduction by Diane Koenker in *Tret'ja vserossijskaja konferencija*, p.XXII: 'Lozovsky appears to have almost single-handedly held the national union movement together after the June Conference'.
38. See, *Sestoj s-ezd RDSRP (b). Avgust 1917g. Protokoly* (Mosow, 1958).
39. I. N. Ljubimov, *Revoljucija 1917 goda. Chronika sobitij. Bd. 6, Oktjabr'-dekabr'* (Moscow and Leningrad, 1930), pp.30, 46, 68, 72, 82. For extracts from his letter, see James Bunyan and H. H. Fischer (eds), *The Bolshevik Revolution 1917–1918. Documents and Materials* (Stanford, CA, 1934), pp.204–6. Further, Daniels, *Conscience of Revolution*, p.66ff; Leonard Schapiro, *The Origin of the Communist Autocracy. Political Opposition in the Soviet State. First Phase 1917–1922* (London, 1955), pp.76–9.
40. Quoted in Maurice Brinton, *The Bolsheviks and Workers' Control* (1970), reprinted in *For Workers' Power. The Sekected Writings of Maurice Brinton*, Edinburgh-Oakland 2004, pp.203–378, here p.328.
41. See the extracts of the discussion in the CEC reproduced in Bunyan and Fisher (eds), *Bolshevik Revolution*, pp.380–4.
42. See, Ljubimov, *Revoljucija, vol.6*, pp.124, 142, 229; Carmen Sirianni, *Workers' Control and Socialist Democracy: The Soviet Experience in Comparative Perspective* (London, 1982), p.97; Brügmann, *Die russischen Gewerkschaften*, pp.123–7 (for an exposition on Losovsky's criticisms of the October revolution); Frederick I. Kaplan, *Bolshevik Ideology and the Ethics of Soviet Labour. 1917–1920: The Formative Years* (London, 1969), pp.172, 197–202, 219–21.
43. Nadeshda Krupskaja, *Erinnerungen an Lenin* (Berlin-DDR, 1959), p.471. In the English edition, the final part on the October revolution is missing as it was written as a later addendum.
44. S. A. Lozovskij, *Rabočij kontrol'* (Petrograd, 1918). See, also, the summary in S. A. Smith, *Red Petrograd. Revolution in the factories 1917–18* (Cambridge, 1985), pp.214–16.
45. Bunyan and Fisher, *Bolshevik Revolution*, p.313.
46. For more details, see Lenin's draft of the resolution on Lozovsky's expulsion in, *Collected Works*, vol.42 (Moscow, 1971), pp.49–51.
47. Bunyan and Fisher give the date of his expulsion as 11.1.[24.1] 1918, rather than 30.12.1917 [12.1.1918], see *Bolshevik Revolution*, pp.637ff.
48. On the First Congress, in addition to the protocol (Protokoll Pervyj s-ezd 1918), see Brügmann, *Die russischen Gewerkschaften*, pp.158–72. For excerpts for the congress and its resolutions, see Bunyan and Fisher (eds), *Bolshevik Revolution*, pp.638–42.
49. *Pervyj s-ezd* 1918, pp.38, 97.
50. *Vtoroj vserossijskij s-ezd professional'nych sojuzov. 16–25 janvarja 1919 goda. Stenograficeskij otcet* (Moscow, 1921).
51. These details are taken from his biography in *Bjulleten' Krasnogo Internacionala Profsojuzov*, Nr. 37–38, 1.8.1921.

52. See King, 'Between Bolshevism and Menshevism'.
53. Victor Serge, *Year One of the Russian Revolution* (Chicago, 1972), p.199.
54. S.A. Dridzo-Lozovskij, *Oktjabr'skaja revoljucija i professional'nye sojuzy* (Moscow, 1919).
55. *Vos'moj s-ezd RKP (b). Mart 1919goda. Protokoly* (Moscow, 1959), pp.33ff.
56. In early 1920, Lozovsky presented an obviously exaggerated picture of the 'Social Democratic Internationalists', which claimed that they had enjoyed 'rather extensive influence' in the trade unions, especially in the leather and railway workers' unions. See, A. Losowski, *Die Gewerkschaften in Sowjetrussland* (Berlin, 1920), p.97.
57. In a further article, this period in his life in the RILU will be presented in more detail. The research this concluding section rests upon can be read in, Reiner Tosstorff, *Profintern: Die Rote Gewerkschaftsinternationale 1920–1937* (Paderborn, 2004).

Vladimir Aleksandrovich Bazarov (1874–1939)
One of the first dissident communists

Francis King

If we take the term 'communism' to refer to the movement that originated in the Bolshevik faction of Russian social democracy from 1903 onwards, then Vladimir Aleksandrovich Rudnev (V. Bazarov) must count as one of the first dissident communists. His entire intellectual career, spanning more than four decades, was characterised by a free-thinking scepticism. This was even reflected in his choice of *nom-de-plume*: the original 'Bazarov' was a character in Turgenev's *Fathers and Sons*, noted for his independence of thought and his unwillingness to bow to authority.

Vladimir Rudnev was born in Tula on 25 July (6 August) 1874. His father, Aleksandr Matveevich Rudnev, was the senior doctor in the local municipal hospital. Vladimir received a good education at the Tula Classical Gymnasium, which gave him a working knowledge of German, French, English, Ancient Greek and Latin. He then went to Moscow University to study chemistry, where he became involved with revolutionary student circles.[1]

It was at this time that he formed a close intellectual relationship with A. A. Malinovsky (1873–1928, later better known as Bogdanov), who was studying in the same faculty. The friendship between Rudnev and Malinovsky-Bogdanov lasted until the latter's death, and was of decisive importance in shaping Rudnev's political and philosophical views. Like many Russian revolutionaries at that time, they began as narodnik socialists before gravitating towards Marxism. According to Bogdanov, it was not until the beginning of 1896 that they both arrived at a definite Marxist position.[2] Within months, they were lecturing to groups of workers at the Tula munitions factory, organised by I.I. Savel'ev, a munitions worker and the founder of the Tula social-democratic organisation.[3] One of the main subjects discussed was political economy, which obliged Rudnev and Bogdanov to make a detailed study of Marx's economics. Bogdanov's study materials were published in 1897 as *Kratkiy kurs ekonomicheskoy nauki*, later reissued in English translation as *A Short Course of Economic Science* (London,

1923). Rudnev's researches also resulted in a book: V. Bazarov, *Productive and Value-Creating Labour* (St Petersburg, 1899). This was the first time he used the pseudonym by which he later became generally known.

This first book was a critical discussion of inconsistencies in Marx's conception of productive and unproductive labour. In Volume 1 of *Capital* Marx had written that 'that labourer alone is productive, who produces surplus value for the capitalist', whether that labour was employed in producing material goods or services.[4] However, in Volume 2 of *Capital*, Marx had argued that labour employed in the trade and banking sectors was neither productive nor value-producing, and that the costs of circulation incurred in these sectors represented 'a deduction of surplus value or surplus product'.[5] The transport of commodities, on the other hand, *was* regarded by Marx as productive, value-adding labour, as it is a necessary condition for their use-values to be realised in the process of consumption. Bazarov argued that this conception led to 'certain inexactitudes and contradictions which…prevent Marx and Engels' system from acquiring a fully harmonious and complete form', in that it could not explain how merchant capital not only manages to recoup its 'unproductive' costs, but even manages to make profit at the normal rate in the given economy.[6]

The solution Bazarov proposed was simple: if the process of production was considered on the level of the whole economy, then it could be regarded as 'the whole set of manipulations which are socially necessary for an object of nature to become an object of consumption'.[7] The criterion of social necessity is historically defined. In a capitalist economy, alongside the processes traditionally considered 'productive', trade, banking, and various other manipulations are essential to the functioning of the economic mechanism. Thus the costs of circulation only belong to Marx's *faux frais* of production if they exceed the socially-necessary norm—just like any other costs incurred in production.

This early book displayed certain features which characterised Bazarov's approach for the next forty years. Even Marx, for whom he had the greatest respect, was not an unchallengeable authority. Marxism, to Bazarov, represented a scientific method, rather than a revealed truth to be defended against heresy. It showed that he had a thorough grasp of Marx's ideas, and could assess them critically. More specifically, the notion that the economy should be seen as an interconnected whole and analysed as such was to become a central theme of his subsequent work in the Soviet planning apparatus.

In 1899 he was exiled for his political activities to Kaluga, along with Bogdanov. In Kaluga they both made the acquaintance of A.V. Lunacharsky

(1875–1933). The three of them were to co-operate closely for the next decade or so. Bazarov left Kaluga in 1900 to study at Berlin University, where he met his wife-to-be, Evgeniya Margolina. In Berlin he was involved in a social-democratic circle that attempted to bridge the ideological gulf that had opened in the RSDRP between the 'economists', who saw the workers' economic struggles as the most important field of activity for socialists, and the *Iskra* group, which placed far more emphasis on political struggles. In 1901 he returned to Russia, and joined the Moscow Committee of the RSDRP, following the arrest of its previous membership. This renewed committee was also arrested at its first meeting on 27 September 1901.[8] Prior to being exiled for three years to Eastern Siberia in 1902, he married Evgeniya in the prison chapel, so that she could be with him in exile. Until early 1905 they lived in a village on the river Chulym, and he earned money translating political and philosophical works from German and French. Their son Aleksandr was born there in 1903.

During this time, Bogdanov and Lunacharsky resided in Vologda, which was to prove highly significant for the ideological evolution of the whole group. In 1902, the intellectual debates of the Vologda political exiles revolved around the ideas of Nikolay Berdyaev (1874–1948), an ex-Marxist who was moving via the ideas of Kant to a form of Christian idealism of his own invention. Bogdanov and Lunacharsky immediately set about organising rival study circles to the Berdyaev groups, and engaged Berdyaev in ideological and philosophical battle. Bazarov, from distant Siberia, also took part in developing the ideas which, Bogdanov and Lunacharsky later claimed, were so effective in undermining Berdyaev's influence among the Vologda exiles.[9] This was the combination of empiricist epistemology ('empiriocriticism') and Marxist collectivism which became the hallmark of the Bogdanov group.[10]

At the end of 1903 the RSDRP, at its second congress in London, split into two factions over a clause in the rules on conditions of party membership. Communication problems meant that this division into Bolsheviks and Mensheviks took a little time to become known throughout the RSDRP. By early 1904 Bogdanov, Lunacharsky and Bazarov had identified themselves with the Bolshevik side, and Lenin, desperately short of supporters, welcomed this influx of literary and political talent, despite his reservations about their philosophical orientation.[11] At this stage the Bolsheviks were the more ideologically heterodox of the two main RSDRP factions. The Mensheviks used this fact as ammunition in the factional struggle: as early as November 1904, Lyubov' Aksel'rod-Ortodoks (1868–1946) criticised the attempt to combine empiriocritical philosophy and Marxism as a 'new variety of revisionism' in the Menshevik-controlled newspaper *Iskra*.[12]

Around the beginning of 1905 Bazarov returned from exile to St. Petersburg, and immediately got involved in the Petersburg Committee of the RSDRP. He was arrested again in June and expelled from the city, but he returned after the Tsar's October 1905 amnesty, just as the events of 1905 were reaching their culmination.[13] His main sphere of activity continued to be literary work—he was on the editorial board of the Bolshevik journal *Proletariy*, and following the reunification of the RSDRP in December 1905, he became one of the Bolshevik representatives on the editorial board of the central RSDRP organ, *Sotsial-Demokrat*. He collaborated on the Petersburg Bolshevik press, legal and illegal. At the Unification Congress of the RSDRP in Stockholm in April 1906, he chaired the congress commission on uniting the various national social-democratic organisations.[14] For a brief period he was also a member of the 'Bolshevik Centre', the factional leadership formed during the Fifth RSDRP Congress in May 1907.[15]

During this time Bazarov was also prolific in the wider literary sphere. His philosophical writings ranged over a wide area, from literary criticism, to surveys of new tendencies in Russian Orthodox theology, to epistemology. On this last question, the theory of knowledge, Bazarov followed Bogdanov in attempting to overcome the 'dualism' they perceived in Marxist materialism as expounded by G.V. Plekhanov (1856–1918), which distinguished between things, on the one hand, and people's perceptions of them, on the other. The Bogdanov school believed that ideas on the philosophy of science recently developed by the Austrian physicist Ernst Mach (1838–1916), enabled them to eliminate the distinction between 'things in themselves' and people's sense data, by redefining objective reality as 'socially-organised experience'. Plekhanov, who was the leading authority on Marxist philosophy not only in Russia, but throughout the European social-democratic movement, responded to these attempts to mix Marx and Mach with magisterial scorn.

However, arguably Bazarov's most important original work from this period had little to do with philosophy. His *Anarchist Communism and Marxism*, published in 1906, contained some ideas about the very nature of socialism which he was subsequently to develop much further. As a critique of anarchism, Bazarov's book did not go beyond the bounds of social-democratic orthodoxy. He accused the anarchists of rationalist utopianism, of elevating tactics to the level of principle, and of seeing history and social development in essentially moral terms, as a struggle between good and evil. However, since anarchism is, above all, a vision of a different society, he was obliged to explore in some detail how the Marxist alternative, socialist society, might work. Social-democrats had traditionally avoided such speculation as 'unscientific', but this, naturally enough, had never impressed anarchists or their sympathisers.

From his reading of Marx, Bazarov regarded it as axiomatic that 'the basis of social development is the growth of productive forces', and that 'a fall in the labour cost of articles of consumption is the most general result and at the same time an objective regulator of human progress'.[16] It followed that a socialist economy could only replace capitalism if it led to a more efficient organisation of production. But the capitalists themselves were also constantly striving to produce more efficiently. The only potential economic advantage of socialism that was necessarily inaccessible to capitalism lay in removing the inefficiencies associated with the anarchic, unplanned nature of capitalist economy, through planned social regulation of the productive process on an international scale.

However, anarchism's central argument has always been its insistence that state power and individual freedom are incompatible, and the stronger the state power, the greater its potential for oppression becomes. Bazarov had to try to show that the centralised, global planned economy he advocated would, at least eventually, not require any state machine at all. According to Marxist theory, there was, in principle, no problem. The state is an organ for ensuring the domination of one class over another, and thus, he insisted, 'the state is unnecessary and impossible in socialist society, it inevitably dies off with the end of the class struggle'.[17] This reasoning alone would scarcely have convinced many anarchists. He therefore elaborated how he envisaged a socialist economy would function, and why authoritarian power relations and structures would be redundant in such a society. He saw the solution to the problem of how to combine international planning with unconditional freedom in the 'universality of mathematical axioms'.[18]

> In the socialist system any question of productive technique becomes a mathematical task of a given type, moreover it is a task the correct solution of which is in the interests of everyone involved in production without exception…The correctness of a mathematical conclusion can be established neither by decrees, nor by universal ballots…[19]

An implicit assumption here, which Bazarov did not attempt to explore, was that there was only one line of social and economic development that could be considered optimal; all the alternatives were objectively, and demonstrably, inferior. This notion of a single optimal line of development was to re-emerge in his writings on planning in the 1920s.

From 1907 to 1909 Bazarov and I.I. Skvortsov-Stepanov (1870–1928) were completing their largest ever translation project—all three volumes of Marx's *Capital*. Their translation remains the basis of the standard Russian-language version. The surviving correspondence between Bazarov and Skvortsov-Stepanov shows that translation work of this type was an important source of income at this time.[20] In 1908 Bazarov's second child, a daughter, Anastasia, was born. At this time he was maintaining an intensive output of philosophical essays, publishing six fairly lengthy pieces in a variety of anthologies, on such subjects as literary criticism, Marxist philosophy and new developments in religion.

The year 1908 also saw the dispute within the Bolshevik faction over philosophy begin to come to a head. Lenin had been increasingly embarrassed by the fact that Plekhanov, who was siding with the Mensheviks in the RSDRP's main factional dispute, was able to use the heterodoxy of the Bogdanov group to discredit the Bolshevik side. In April 1908 A.M. Gorky invited Bazarov, Bogdanov, Lunacharsky, along with Lenin and others to Capri, where he was then living. This gathering amounted to a congress of Bolshevik writers, and philosophical questions were the main focus of discussion. The gulf between the Leninists and the adherents of empiriocriticism and 'empiriomonism' proved quite unbridgeable, and from then on the split within the Bolshevik faction widened, with increasingly spirited polemics from both sides. This split was a complex affair, since the lines of fracture in philosophical matters did not correspond to the divisions on attitudes to such questions as the Duma elections, or relations with the Mensheviks. Bazarov, for example, unlike Bogdanov and Lunacharsky, agreed with Lenin after June 1907 that social-democrats should participate in elections to the Duma.[21] Bazarov did not play a significant role in the wrangling around the break between Bogdanov's and Lenin's groups. He had ceased to be a member of the 'Bolshevik Centre', the faction's leading body, some time before Lenin and Bogdanov finally parted ways in June 1909. By this time Bazarov was active primarily as a publicist, and as a member of the literary group of the Moscow Committee of the RSDRP.

Bazarov did not join the group of 'left Bolsheviks' around the newspaper *Vpered*, nor did he lecture at the left-Bolshevik political schools organised by Bogdanov on Capri in 1909, or in Bologna in 1910. He remained a member of the RSDRP, considered himself to be a Bolshevik, although not a Leninist, and clearly did not feel bound by the decisions of any factional committee. His literary and political connections transcended many of the normal boundaries within Russian socialism, and in 1910 he even wrote for

A.N. Potresov's 'Menshevik-liquidationist' journal *Nasha zarya*.

Bazarov was arrested again in 1911 for contacts with RSDRP comrades abroad, and exiled to Astrakhan' gubernia, where he stayed until shortly before the outbreak of war in 1914. On leaving Astrakhan' he returned to St. Petersburg, where he was to remain until mid-1918.

In 1913, V. Bazarov contributed a series of articles on the 'Philosophy of Action' to the journal *Sovremennik*, then edited by the Socialist-Revolutionary leader Viktor Chernov (1873–1952). Shortly thereafter, Chernov was replaced by Nikolay Sukhanov (1882–1940), with whom Bazarov was to work closely for the next fifteen years. In 1915 he published two further articles 'On the Current Ideological Crisis' in *Sovremennik*. At the end of 1915 Gorky founded the journal *Letopis'*, virtually the only periodical then legally published in Russia that took an internationalist attitude to the war. Its style and content ensured that the bulk of its readership came from the intelligentsia. Its regular contributors included Bazarov, Sukhanov, B.V. Avilov (1874–1938) and A.N. Tikhonov (1880–1956).

The overthrow of Tsarism in February 1917 caused Bazarov to reorientate his activity as a journalist, and to write for a mass audience rather than just for intellectuals. Within a few days of Tsar Nicholas II's abdication, the Petersburg Soviet had been refounded. Sukhanov, who had attended one of its sessions almost accidentally, was appointed to the Soviet's literary commission, which was given the task of founding the Soviet newspaper, *Izvestiya Petrogradskogo Soveta Rabochikh Deputatov*. Sukhanov recruited many of his *Letopis'* colleagues, including Bazarov, to the first *Izvestiya* editorial group.[22] However, his main contribution to the work of the Petrograd Soviet was in its Economic Section, founded on the initiative of the Menshevik Vladimir Groman (1874–1932), which drew up the Soviet's programme for the regulation of production and distribution. This marked the beginning of thirteen years' collaboration between Bazarov and Groman.[23]

In the course of 1917, Bazarov developed the view that wartime economic regulation, with its state syndication of capitalist enterprises and state organisation and control of production ('state capitalism') were not just crisis-management measures, but a new phase in the organisation of capitalist economy, the specific form of capitalism in its imperialist phase. However, unlike Lenin, he did not see it as an *immediate* precursor to socialism. In June 1917 he predicted that 'this "military" organisation of production' would expand further after the war, as no other system would be able to cope with demobilising the world economy. Although he believed that it was 'the first step in a process of political and social transformation which can only be completed by the introduction of the socialist system', he expected this new phase to last for some considerable time. Consequently, he argued that for the time being in Russia, 'our form of regulation should retain its state capitalist character'.²⁴ In subsequent months Bazarov developed this conception of state capitalism further, arguing that as it had not exhausted its potential for developing productive forces, it was 'guaranteed a more or less lengthy existence'. However, in the context of the Russian revolution, it could serve as 'that practical school of socialism necessary for the social reeducation of the proletariat itself'. The chance to participate in running and planning this type of economy could help working people become 'the free and responsible organisers of socialist production'.²⁵ This approach could supersede Engels's well-known description of the socialist revolution as a 'leap from the realm of necessity into the realm of freedom',²⁶ which, Bazarov acknowledged, had been 'characterised by Marxism's enemies—not without reason—as a belief in social miracles'.²⁷

In the first weeks after the February revolution, Bazarov had attempted to work within his old faction. The Bolshevik memoirist A.G. Shlyapnikov recalled that 'during the first days of the [February] revolution the former Bolshevik Bazarov played a fairly active part in the meetings of our faction at the Soviet, and together with [B.V.] Avilov constituted its right wing'.²⁸ Shlyapnikov summarised their line thus:

> This group advocated a platform of all-party agreements, favoured support for the Provisional Government and controlling it through the Soviet. In relation to the war Avilov and Bazarov took positions similar to the Soviet's call 'To the peoples of all countries' and opposed advancing the 'naked slogan—down with the war!'²⁹

This approach found little favour among the Petrograd Bolsheviks even before Lenin's return from Switzerland. The break was completed by Lenin's uncompromising radicalism in 1917, as expressed in his 'April Theses'. According to Sukhanov, about five days after his return from exile Lenin called a meeting to establish the political attitudes of some of the most able Bolshevik figures from the 1905 period, including Avilov, Bazarov and V. Stroev-Desnitsky (1878–1958). Not one of them was prepared to accept Lenin's radical line.³⁰

In April 1917 Bazarov was one of those recruited by Gorky to work on his new newspaper *Novaya zhizn'*. Other regular contributors included Sukhanov, Avilov, Stroev, G.D. Lindov-Leiteizen (1874–1919), Rafail Grigor'ev (1889–1968), and A.N. Tikhonov. This well-informed and widely-read newspaper adopted a social-democratic, internationalist editorial line, but at first stood apart from any particular faction within the RSDRP. In May 1917 Bazarov was calling for the broadest possible realignment of Russian socialism, on the grounds that all the factional and even party delineations had become redundant:

> The socialists are currently divided into factions, which do not always correspond even to their general policies. 'Bolshevik', 'Menshevik', 'Socialist-Revolutionary'—to a considerable extent these are historical relics; the actual programmatic differences between Russian socialists do not fit into these divisions bequeathed to us from the past.[31]

In general, though, *Novaya zhizn'* paid little attention to the SRs, and concentrated on Russian social-democracy. The paper wanted the internationalists in the RSDRP, from whatever faction, to unite into a single internationalist social-democratic party which would exclude the defencist Mensheviks on the right, and marginalise the uncompromising Leninists on the far left. Bazarov and his colleagues initially had high hopes for the RSDRP 'unification conference' in August 1917, but the result was a great disappointment for them. The Bolsheviks did not take part, and the conference served merely to paper over the differences between internationalist and defencist Mensheviks. The bulk of the internationalists, whatever their reservations about Leninism, remained with the Bolsheviks. *Novaya zhizn'* then tried to serve as an alternative pole of attraction by setting up a separate group called the United Social-Democrat Internationalists (US-DI). The founding statements and documents of this group, which were formally adopted at a conference one week before the Bolsheviks seized power in October 1917, were largely drafted by Bazarov.[32] Overall, its policies and approach were indistinguishable from those of the Menshevik-Internationalists, except that they refused to be in the same party as the Menshevik-defencists. However, although the US-DI were opposed to the Bolshevik takeover, and to the whole notion of 'Soviet power', they did not follow Yu. O. Martov (1873–1923) out of the Second All-Russian Congress of Soviets, and for six days after the Congress Bazarov was one of the US-DI representatives on the Soviet Central Executive Committee (TsIK). The US-DI withdrew its representatives only once the Bolsheviks had refused to form a broad coalition government with the other socialist parties.

The US-DI changed its title in January 1918 to the RSDRP (internationalists). It soon began to disintegrate. Its left wing, led by Alexander Lozovsky (1878–1952) was gradually absorbed into the Bolsheviks throughout 1918 and 1919. The right wing, including Bazarov, Avilov, Stroev-Desnitsky and

Grigor'ev, controlled *Novaya zhizn'*, which became increasingly hostile to the Bolshevik regime during 1918 as the economy collapsed, repression intensified, and civil war and foreign intervention began. This group left the RSDRP(i) around the middle of 1918, and when the Bolshevik authorities closed *Novaya zhizn'* in July 1918, its writers went their separate ways. Most of them eventually found work in various Soviet institutions.

In the summer of 1918 Bazarov left Petrograd, and in early 1919 he lived in Khar'kov, where he collaborated with Martov and others to publish *Mysl'*, a weekly political journal of a Menshevik orientation. Bazarov published several articles in fourteen issues of *Mysl'*, in which he analysed and commented on the progress of the Bolshevik regime. This was the period of 'war communism', in which the Soviet authorities attempted to run the entire economy by administrative means, and which was both a response to, and a cause of, the economy's unprecedentedly rapid collapse at that time. Given Bazarov's identification of progress with the development of productive forces, it is not surprising that his attitude was very hostile. The alternative measures he proposed were very similar to those the Soviet government was forced to accept after 1921: a 'natural tax per *desyatina*' on the peasants in place of requisitioning,[33] and rationalisation of industry under state control. He also lampooned the Bolsheviks' pretensions to lead the world revolutionary movement as 'the most profound and complete manifestation of Russian messianism', and compared the 'Third International' to the obscurantist Slavophile notion of Moscow as the 'Third Rome'.[34]

Later in 1919, Bazarov headed south to join his family in the Crimea, where his mother-in-law lived. There he found work lecturing to workers and students and writing for the trade-union press. Once the Red Army had taken the Crimea, the family were held under house arrest for a period. On 25 January 1921 Gorky raised the case of the Rudnev family with Lenin. Shortly thereafter they were released from house arrest and invited to live in Moscow.[35] After a short time employed as an economist at the Socialist Academy, Bazarov started work at the newly-created State Planning Commission, Gosplan, on 1 May 1921.

Although he had lost his political independence, the period from 1921 to the end of 1927 represented the pinnacle of Bazarov's real influence and authority. Gosplan, like other central Soviet economic bodies, had recruited a talented group of economists who were non-communist socialists of various types. They were prepared to forgo some of their political freedom in return for the opportunity to remain in Russia and help practically in its reconstruction. Moreover, unlike war communism, the 'New Economic Policy' (NEP) represented an economic approach they could support. The most important members of this group were Bazarov and V.G. Groman. Although their political backgrounds were different—Groman had been a Menshevik and, until 1917, not a particularly radical one—on questions of economic policy and planning in the 1920s Bazarov and Groman were almost invariably in agreement. This was partly because both had been strongly influenced by Bogdanov's conception of a 'universal organisational science' (Tektology), which regarded the economy as a single interconnected system in dynamic equilibrium, operating according to laws which were analogous to laws found in nature.[36]

Both Bazarov and Groman worked in the statistical-economic section of Gosplan. This section was concerned above all with collecting, collating and analysing economic data, and evolving methods for forecasting and, ultimately, planning economic development. Gosplan was attached to the Council of Labour and Defence (STO), one of the most important administrative and executive bodies in the Soviet state apparatus, and Bazarov frequently acted as a consultant from Gosplan to the deliberations both of the STO, and of the government. He held various responsible positions in the time he worked in Gosplan—as deputy director of the economic-statistical section from 1924, and as a member of the presidium of Gosplan's economic sector from the end of 1926. In June 1927 he was appointed as a member of the Gosplan presidium. Together with Stanislav G. Strumilin (1877–1974), Bazarov and Groman were responsible for compiling Gosplan's annual 'control figures' for 1925–26, 1926–27 and 1927–28—the first plans ever compiled for the Soviet economy as a whole.[37]

During this period Bazarov published extensively. He helped found the journal *Ekonomicheskoe obozrenie* ('Economic Survey') in 1923, and was until 1926 one of its editors. He contributed regularly to that journal, and to *Planovoye khozyaystvo* ('Planned Economy'), the magazine of Gosplan. His articles ranged over a wide subject area, but his speciality was methodological problems in economic planning. In the early years of NEP he wrote extensively on inflationary processes, later he paid a lot of attention to general and specific problems in devising perspective (longer-range) plans for economic development. He coined the terms 'genetics' and 'teleology' to denote, respectively, planning on the basis of past performance and planning on the basis of policy directive, and insisted that a plan needed to contain an organic synthesis of the two methods. He analysed the tempo of economic reconstruction in the USSR under NEP. Along with Groman, he advanced the view that this tempo, plotted on a graph, would produce something akin to an S-shaped curve. Recovery after 1921 had initially been relatively slow, but had then accelerated rapidly around 1924–25, following the currency reform and the end of hyperinflation. Bazarov and Groman predicted that Soviet economic growth would slow down again once the pre-existing capital was brought fully back into operation and output approached the pre-war level. In a major work published in 1927, Bazarov analysed this recovery process and compared its structure with that of capitalist trade cycles.[38]

Work as a Gosplan economist not only gave Bazarov the opportunity to examine economic trends and suggest policy options, but also to participate in a practical way in laying the foundations on which, he hoped, a new, socialist society could be built. He envisaged a gradual, long-term process, in which a planned economy would emerge through the perfection of economic techniques and the rise in the cultural level of the population. In 1928 he described the basic aims of long-range planning as follows: 'an optimal combination of the growth of productive forces, an increase in the living standards of the workers and the development of the processes of socialisation constitute the teleological pivot of the plan; the postulate of 'crisis-free reproduction' determines the methodology.'[39] He insisted that 'the development of the productive forces is the leading link', and could envisage no circumstances where the growth of productive forces should be subordinated to an increase in living standards or the development of socialisation.[40] Indeed, if sectors of the economy were socialised before they were ready for it, and the growth of productive forces were thereby fettered, this 'would discredit the very principle of socialisation'.[41]

Bazarov saw the development of planning techniques, giving humanity the ability collectively to control and direct economic processes, as an essential prerequisite for any eventual victory of socialism as a social system—the cause to which he had devoted his entire adult life. This did not mean that he had become reconciled to the one-party dictatorship, censorship, crude repression or other aspects of Bolshevik practice he had criticised after 1917. He collaborated with the Soviet authorities in pursuit of a common goal, a planned economy. His writings in the 1920s were refreshingly free from Soviet political clichés and ritual verbiage. Unlike many of his colleagues, he was clearly not remotely in awe of the CPSU leaders. Bazarov belonged to the same generation as Lenin, and in the early years of the Bolshevik faction had been one of his colleagues rather than one of his followers. In the course of a discussion on the Five-Year plan organised at the Communist Academy in 1928, Bazarov reminded his audience ironically about 'one old communist who has, unfortunately, been rather overlooked in our country recently, although in his time he enjoyed great authority, no less, indeed, than Stalin, Bukharin and other outstanding communists enjoy today. I am thinking of

Karl Marx....'⁴² Indeed, by 1928, the only Bolshevik whose knowledge and understanding of Marx could rival that of Bazarov was the director of the Marx-Engels Institute, David Ryazanov (1870–1938).

Overall, during the NEP period Bazarov was undoubtedly influential—but only as long as his economic ideas remained compatible with the policies of the communist party leadership, which meant, in effect, the relatively cautious approach of the Bukharin group. When Stalin moved against Bukharin and his line after 1928, Bazarov, Groman and the other non-party economists in Gosplan and other economic institutions rapidly lost their influence. Moreover, the Stalin group's use of the First Five-Year Plan not as a scientific guide, but as a mobilisation and propaganda tool, represented a decisive rejection of the previous approach to planning.

In the course of the crash industrialisation and collectivisation, the hardships and failures of those years were blamed on 'wreckers', allegedly working on behalf of the class enemy in Soviet institutions. Several show trials of 'wreckers' were held between 1928 and 1933, and 'wrecking' was used to describe not just physical sabotage, but ideological sabotage as well. Many leading non-party economists, including Bazarov, were arrested in the autumn of 1930. These arrests were preceded and followed by an increasingly vehement campaign against 'bourgeois' and 'Mensheviks' in the planning apparatus. Almost any planner who had publicly expressed doubts about the feasibility of the ever-increasing output targets proposed in each new variant of the First Five-Year Plan fell into these categories.

The show trial of the 'All-Union Bureau of Mensheviks' opened on 1 March 1931. There were fourteen defendants, most of them Bazarov's friends and colleagues, including Groman and Sukhanov. Groman's testimony directly implicated Bazarov as the author of the All-Union Bureau's programme. All fourteen pleaded guilty to baseless charges of economic and political sabotage in league with the Menshevik exiles, the Labour and Socialist International and Anglo-French imperialism; all were sentenced to long periods of imprisonment, and only one or two survived to be released after 1956. However, these fourteen had been chosen from a total of 122 persons arrested in connection with the case, many of whom, including Bazarov, refused to admit any guilt.⁴³ This refusal proved to be to his advantage. Unlike his luckless colleagues who confessed, he did not remain in prison for long. He was released around the beginning of 1932, was exiled to Saratov for about eighteen months, and then went to live with his son at a meteorological station near the town of Gagra, in the Caucasus. In May 1935, following his son's accidental death in a snow avalanche, Bazarov was permitted to return to Moscow.

Bazarov was not, however, rehabilitated, and was not allowed to return to his old employment. His arrest had also meant that his wife Evgeniya was sacked from the Commissariat for Education. During the 1930s both Bazarov and Evgeniya Rudneva earned their living translating literary and philosophical works, particularly for the Academia publishing house, then headed by Bazarov's old *Novaya zhizn'* colleague A.N. Tikhonov. Remarkably, in view of his past, Bazarov managed to avoid being swept up in the Great Terror of 1936–38, and died a natural death. For many years, he had suffered from bronchial asthma and in September 1939 he contracted pneumonia. He died at home on 16 September. His wife's fate was more tragic: Evgeniya Rudneva was arrested six days after the German invasion of the USSR in 1941, and died in a labour camp near Sol'-Iletsk in November 1942. She was posthumously rehabilitated in 1957.

Notes

1. Much of the biographical information was taken from a memoir by Bazarov's grandson, E.A. Rudnev, *Moy ded—V.A. Bazarov*, previously obtainable on http://www.bogdinst.ru/vestnik/v12.htm.
2. A. Bogdanov, 'Moe prebyvanie v Tule', in *Revolyutsionnoe byloe*, No.2 (Tula, 1923), p.17.
3. See Bogdanov, op. cit. pp.16–18, and Z.P. Kozyreva et al. (eds) *Istoriya Tul'skogo oruzheynogo zavoda 1812–1972* (Tula, 1973), pp.92–3.
4. Karl Marx, *Capital*, Volume 1 (London, 1891), p.517.
5. Karl Marx, *Capital*, Volume 2 (Harmondsworth, 1978), p.226.
6. V. Bazarov, *Trud proizvoditel'nyy i trud, obrazuyushchiy tsennost'*, (St Petersburg, 1899), p.5.
7. Bazarov, *Trud proizvoditel'nyy*, p.37.
8. See V.I. Nevsky (ed.), *Deyateli revolyutsionnogo dvizheniya v Rossii—bio-bibliograficheskiy slovar', tom pyatyy—sotsial-demokraty 1880–904, vypusk 1, A–B* (Moscow, 1931), pp.192–3.
9. See Robert C. Williams, *The Other Bolsheviks—Lenin and his Critics 1904–1914* (Bloomington, 1986), pp.33, 38.
10. For a detailed account of Bazarov's philosophical ideas and where he fitted into the debates within Russian Marxism, see Daehee Choi, *Politik und Philosophie bei Vladimir A. Bazarov: sein Begriff des Kollektivismus als Konzept der Sozial und Kulturrevolution* (Regensburg, 2000).
11. Choi, *Politik und Philosophie*, p.37.
12. See Ortodoks, 'Novaya raznovidnost' revizionizma', *Iskra*, No.77, 5 November, 1904.
13. Nevsky, *Deyateli revolyutsionnogo dvizheniya v Rossii*, p.193.
14. See *Chetvertyy (ob'edinitel'nyy) s'ezd RSDRP—protokoly* (Moscow, 1959), pp.422–4.

15. Nevsky, op.cit, p.193.
16. V. Bazarov, *Anarkhicheskiy kommunizm i marksizm* (St. Petersburg, 1906), pp.75, 76.
17. ibid., p.11.
18. ibid., p.166.
19. ibid., p.165–6.
20. Russian state Archive of Social and Political History (henceforth: RGASPI), fond 150 (Skvortsov-Stepanov), opis' 1, ed. khr. 112.
21. Nevsky, op.cit., p.193.
22. N. N. Sukhanov, *Zapiski o revolyutsii*, Vol.1 (Moscow, 1991), p.100; Tsuyoshi Hasegawa, *The February Revolution: Petrograd 1917* (Seattle, 1981), p.343.
23. See Sukhanov, op.cit., Vol.1, p.205
24. V. Bazarov, 'Russkaya revolyutsiya i sotsializm', *Novaya zhizn'*, No.39, 3–16 June 1917, p.1.
25. V. Bazarov, 'Perspektivy mirovoy revolyutsii', *Novaya zhizn'*, No.251, 8 March 1918, p.2.
26. Friedrich Engels, *Anti-Dühring* (Peking, 1976), p.367.
27. V. Bazarov, 'Perspektivy mirovoy revolyutsii', *Novaya zhizn'*, No.251, 8 March 1918, p.2.
28. A. G. Shlyapnikov, *Semnadtsatyy god*, Vol.2 (Moscow, 1925), p.186.
29. ibid., p.187.
30. Sukhanov, op.cit., Vol.2, p.20.
31. V. Bazarov, 'Gorodskie vybory i sotsialisticheskie partii', *Novaya zhizn'*, No.15, 5–18 May 1917, p.1.
32. RGASPI, fond 444, op.1, delo 8, l. 8.
33. V. Bazarov, 'Posledniy s'ezd bol'shevikov i zadachi "tekushchego momenta", *Mysl'* No.10, 1919.
34. See V. Bazarov, 'Tretiy Rim i Tretiy International', *Mysl'*, 12, 1919.
35. See *Biograficheskaya khronika Lenina*, Vol.10 (Moscow, 1979), pp.7–8.
36. See G. Gloveli, introduction to A. Bogdanov, *Tektologiya: Vseobshchaya organizatsionnaya nauka* (Moscow, 2003), pp.6–9.
37. The best and most detailed published accounts in English of Bazarov's economic ideas all appeared several decades ago, but remain unsurpassed, see Alexander Erlich, *The Soviet Industrialization Debate, 1924–1928* (Harvard: Cambridge MA, 1960); Nicolas Spulber, *Foundations of Soviet Strategy for Economic Growth—Selected Soviet Essays 1924–1930* (Bloomington, 1964); idem, *Soviet Strategy for Economic Growth* (Bloomington, 1964); Naum Jasny, *Soviet Economists of the Twenties—Names to be Remembered* (Cambridge, 1972).
38. See V. Bazarov, *Kapitalisticheskie tsikly i vosstanovitel'nyy protsess khozyaystva SSSR* (Moscow, 1927).
39. V. Bazarov, 'Printsipy postroeniya perspektivnogo plana', *Planovoe khozyaystvo*, No.2, 1928, p.41.
40. ibid., p.43.
41. ibid., p.42. Bazarov used two Russian terms for 'socialisation', *obobshchestvlenie*

and *sotsializatsiya*, more or less interchangeably in this article.
42. See, *O pyatiletnem plane narodnogo khozyaystva* (Moscow, 1928), p.77.
43. See, A.L. Litvin, compiler, *Men'shevistskiy protsess 1931 goda* Vol.2, (Moscow, 1999), pp.388–98 for a full list of arrestees.

Identity and Self-Representation in Irish Communism
The Connolly Column and the Spanish Civil War

Emmet O'Connor

'It is perhaps considered easier by some to fight fascism in Spain, than work in the exceptionally difficult conditions in the South of Ireland'.
Comintern memorandum, 1937[1]

The first thing to say about Irish communist self-representation is that, outside internal party journals and publications on the Spanish Civil War, it hardly exists. This might seem to be a reflection of the weakness of communism in Ireland. Certainly the conventional wisdom is that communists were of no consequence in Irish history. The most acclaimed survey of the political history of twentieth-century Ireland, Lee's *Ireland: 1912–1985*, made just eight passing references to 'communism' in 687 pages, and those references actually dealt with anti-communism.[2] It is true that the communists were rarely numerous, suffered chronic problems of organisation, and found it difficult to sustain branches outside Dublin and Belfast. The first Communist Party of Ireland (CPI), launched in 1921 by James Connolly's precocious son, Roddy, probably had about 50 to 100 active members over most of its short history, and was dissolved in 1924 in favour of Jim Larkin's Irish Worker League. The League began with some 500 supporters, but Larkin used it as little more than a personal soapbox. Following Larkin's break with the Communist International in 1929, Moscow sponsored the Revolutionary Workers' Groups, preparatory to the foundation of the second CPI in 1933. Membership of the Groups peaked in 1932 at 340, and then declined in the face of clerical reaction. The CPI was wound up in neutral Éire when Germany invaded Soviet Russia. The Communist Party in Northern Ireland (CPNI) flourished briefly in the period of Britain's wartime alliance with the Soviet Union, reaching a membership of 1,000 in 1943. By 1949, the roll call was down to 172. Éire communists re-organised in the Irish Workers' League (later Irish Workers' Party) in 1948, and survived in near clandestine circumstances during the height of the cold war.

The northern and southern parties united as the third CPI in 1970, with a combined membership of some 600.[3]

Yet the communists were of remarkable significance in certain phases of radical history. The British intelligence campaign to depict the Irish independence struggle as 'Bolshevist' was not without some basis in fact.[4] Dáil Éireann sought diplomatic recognition and weapons from Soviet Russia in 1921 and socialist republicanism during the Free State era was driven by the interaction of the Irish Republican Army (IRA) and the Comintern. The Workers' Union of Ireland, the second largest Irish general trade union up to 1990, was founded by the Larkins in 1924 as a communist union, and was the biggest anglophone affiliate of the Profintern up to 1929. The wartime CPNI acquired some lasting positions of influence in Belfast trade unionism and communists played a role in the Northern Ireland Civil Rights Association in the 1960s. Communists also made a major contribution to historiography through T.A. Jackson and C. Desmond Greaves, the twin pillars of the James Connolly school of history, which in turn hegemonised Irish radical historiography up to the 1970s.[5] Nonetheless, it is only in relation to the Connolly Column, the name which has become a blanket term for all Irish-born volunteers who served in Spain for the Republic, that communists have received anything approaching due recognition from professional historians or in the public memory.[6]

A shy tradition

A brief review of other communist autobiography will put the Connolly Column material in perspective. Two comrades of the first CPI, Liam O'Flaherty and Jim Phelan, went on to become prolific writers, and among their various autobiographical publications are two volumes which cover the period of their party membership: O'Flaherty's *Shame the Devil* (1934), and *The Name's Phelan* (1948). Both had by then abandoned politics and wrote primarily to earn a crust. Treating their party activities as incidental to jaunty accounts of adventurous lives, neither said much about communism or the CPI *per se*. Indeed O'Flaherty reveals more about the CPI in one of his best-known novels, *The Informer* (1925).

The history of *The Informer* is symptomatic of the way communism has been airbrushed out of the ferment that went into the making of independent Ireland. Set in 1923–4, the plot has Gypo Nolan on the run from 'the Revolutionary Organisation' as it hovers on the brink of becoming a power in the land, in a manner approximate to one of Roddy Connolly's pipedreams during the civil war. The organisation's commandant, Dan

Gallagher, was invested with many of the failings attributed to Connolly by his disgruntled comrades, notably O'Flaherty himself. The novel has inspired four films. A British production in 1929 by Arthur Robison gave the events a vaguely German location. John Ford's 1935 Academy-Award winner shifted the setting to the War of Independence and projected Gypo as a renegade IRA man. The same approach was taken in a 1992 version, while the radical 1968 film *Uptight!* set the story in a black ghetto of urban America. In the 1920s it was possible to believe that O'Flaherty's significance lay in his communism. 'I think if you eliminate Bolshevism and muck-raking from Liam O'Flaherty', wrote Desmond Fitzgerald, the Free State's first Minister for External Affairs, 'you have a very unimportant writer'.[7] Subsequently, it became impossible to think of Irish communism as anything other than esoteric, even in fiction. Gypo Nolan, one of the great examples of the stock villain of native demonology, passed into Irish idiom as a republican traitor, and the most recent academic study of *The Informer* reckoned that Gallagher was inspired by officers of the Bavarian *Frei Korps*.[8]

Communist autobiography in the post-1930s period is confined to published interviews with Betty Sinclair, Joe Deasy, and Andy Barr, which deal primarily with their involvement in trade unionism and politics rather than internal party affairs; private papers in the Desmond Greaves archive; and Roy Johnston's doorstopper, *Century of Endeavour: A Biographical and Autobiographical View of the Twentieth Century in Ireland* (2003).[9] Unique in so many respects, *Century of Endeavour* is a biography of Johnston's father, an Ulster liberal and later a member of the Republic's senate, and a memoir of Roy's involvement in communist and republican groups in Dublin from the 1940s, and in the Connolly Association in London. Presented in the manner of a reconstructed diary, and written in a spare and factual style, it includes an extraordinarily detailed record of meetings and discussions.[10]

That communists have been shy of autobiography is not surprising. Irish political autobiography withered as a genre with the demise of the Home Rule party in 1918. The party's MPs were infused with the élitist, pretentious atmosphere of Westminster. The demotic political culture of independent Ireland reflected a society which was predominently rural, conformist, and consensual, and which esteemed the collective above the personal. The few IRA commandants who published memoirs of the War of Independence aimed primarily to give their version of events rather than observations on themselves or the world about them.[11] There was too a feeling that the post-1921 period, when the Irish quarrelled more with each other, than with the stranger, and when the arrival at statehood failed to match the high expectations of the journey, was not an appropriate subject of scrutiny. None had greater cause for embarrassment than the socialists, who witnessed the exhilarating workers' unity of the Larkinite and syndicalist years crumble into extraordinary fractiousness between 1923 and 1959. When William O'Brien, long-time general secretary of the Irish Transport and General Workers' Union (ITGWU), finally produced a memoir, he refused to go beyond the events of 1923, though he did not retire until 1946.[12] Being mainly working class and imbued with the characteristic secretiveness of their parties, Irish communists felt even less inclined to tell their stories in public. The wonder is not that so few communist autobiographies are available, but that so much has been written in recent years, and written almost entirely in relation to the Spanish Civil War.

'The Spanish trenches are here in Ireland'[13]

Between July 1936 and the summer of 1937 there was no escaping the Spanish question in Ireland.[14] It is possible that *per capita* the Irish accounted for more volunteers in Spain than any other nation. Of course, most fought for General Franco, and many of those on the other side were emigrés. Nonetheless, the level of Irish involvement in the International Brigades was remarkable for a country with a communist party of about 150 members, confined organisationally to Dublin and Belfast. The explanation lies in the way Spain impacted on two forces in Irish society and politics, Catholicism and republicanism. Inflamed by lurid accounts of anti-clerical atrocities, crowds of up to 50,000 thronged the rallies of the Irish Christian Front, formed in August 1936 to support Franco and combat communism. The Irish Catholic hierarchy raised £43,000 in church-gate collections for Spanish Catholics, and backed the creation of an 'Irish Brigade' to fight what it represented as a religious crusade. The brigade was commanded by General Eoin O'Duffy, chief of police from 1922 to 1933, then leader of Ireland's 'shirted' movement, the Blueshirts, and for a time the president of the main opposition party, Fine Gael. About 680 strong, with its own pipe band, it attracted widespread curiosity as the only unit of foreign volunteers in Franco's army other than a scattering of individuals and the state-sponsored auxiliaries from Germany, Italy, and Portugal. Such was the intensity of anti-communist feeling that Irish Labour declined to take a stand on the war. After doing its best to avoid the issue, the Labour Party published a remarkably evasive pamphlet, *Cemeteries of Liberty: Communist and Fascist Dictatorships* (1937), written by party leader William Norton and introduced by O'Brien. Skirting both Spanish and Irish politics, Norton treated Fascism as Nazism, and equated Nazism with Stalinism. Labour, as

Norton would have it, was anti-fascist and anti-communist equally, but not pro- or anti-Franco. The Irish Trade-Union Congress took a similar stance. Even Larkin banned officials of his union from speaking in public on Spain. In some cases, workers in British based unions which funded humanitarian aid to Republican Spain made formal protests or disaffiliated.[15]

The twin pillars of opposition to Franco in the Free State were the CPI and the Republican Congress. Alliance with republicans had been a strategic aim of Comintern policy in Ireland since 1920, and republicans had been providing the cadres for communist fronts in Ireland since 1925. The Republican Congress was formed in April 1934, when leftists abandoned the IRA to launch a 'congress of progressives'. The CPI affiliated to the Congress in September. Within weeks the Congress split over whether to continue as a 'united front' or become a political party. What remained of it was so close to the CPI, and *vice versa*, that both organisations could be said to have shared a mutual 'communist republicanism', which might be encapsulated as a belief in the politics of anti-imperialism at home, and the popular front internationally. Little more than their conviction in the party and the Comintern separated the communists from the Congress. Something of a popular front atmosphere emerged as a few writers, intellectuals, and liberals helped to create groups like Irish Friends of the Spanish Republic, branches of the Left Book Club, socialist theatre guilds, and radical debating societies. A fine example of the spirit is Leslie Daiken's *Good-Bye, Twilight: Songs of Struggle in Ireland*, a collection of seventy-five poems and ballads by forty Irish writers and workers, all 'showing unmistakeably out of the experience of the proletariat, that revolutionary poets, playwrights, and novelists are developing an art which reveals more forces in the world than the love of the lecher and the pride of the Narcissist'.[16] If minor by international standards, this level of bourgeois and intellectual engagement with socialism was novel in Ireland. And it reflected a 'communist republican' politics. It was symptomatic of the centrality of republicanism—and emigration—for Irish socialists, that Daiken, a Dublin Jew, was editor of *Irish Front*, the monthly paper of the London branch of the Republican Congress. Only in Northern Ireland, where the climate was more tolerant in relation to Spain, was it possible to find anti-Franco activism outside the 'communist-republican' rubric, in the form of the Socialist Party, Northern Ireland (SPNI), previously the Belfast branch of the (British) Independent Labour Party, and sections of the Northern Ireland Labour Party.

Republicanism is particularly marked in the composition of the 'Connolly Column'. The CPI decided to contribute to the International Brigades in September 1936, and leaders of the Republican Congress, notably Peadar O'Donnell and Frank Ryan, were instrumental in the recruitment of what was intended to be a distinct Irish unit. O'Duffy's 'Brigade', raised with the encouragement of all that republicans regarded with hostility—Fine Gael, the Blueshirts, the Catholic hierarchy, and the *Irish Independent* newspaper—acted as a stimulus. O'Duffy himself was something of a hate figure for republicans, blamed for the massacre of IRA prisoners at Ballyseedy in 1923 and Garda harassment in his days as chief of police.[17] And having been excommunicated in 1922 and 1931, the IRA was cynical about the theological integrity of clerical politics. In respect of those who left from Ireland, the table below almost certainly understates the proportion of volunteers with an IRA background, who are likely to account for the bulk of unknown affiliations.[18] By contrast, it is possible to be reasonably accurate on the CPI members, and say that the communist percentage was low in comparison with other countries.[19] Most republicans were in a batch of about eighty who went to Spain with Ryan in December 1936. Communists dominated the subsequent trickle of recruits.

The politics of the Connolly Column

Residence before Spain	Total	Known affiliation	Communist (with a previous republican affiliation)	Other republicans	Labour/ socialist (with a previous republican affiliation)	Non-party
Ireland	134	62	29 (13)	22	7(1)	4
London	32	23	14 (7)	6	1	2
Elsewhere	77	39	33 (4)	3	3 (1)	-
Total	243	124	76 (24)	31	11 (2)	6

Note to table: Various lists of the Connolly Column have been compiled on the basis of snippets gleaned from a range of sources, and it is impossible to be exact on figures. All lists include those born in Ireland as, while many of the expatriates were politicised abroad, others were the product of Irish politics, and some, notably those in the London Republican Congress, were still engaged with Ireland. This table does not include second-generation exiles or the 'honorary Irish', foreigners who associated with the Irish in Spain. The total of 243 includes 5 who served with the POUM, the CNT, or the Madrid militia, 5 who served in medical units, and 1 driver on a supply convoy. The others were International Brigaders. 'Communist' refers to membership of any communist party before Spain. 'Previous republican affiliation' means former membership of the Citizen Army, IRA, or Republican Congress. 'Labour/socialist' includes an anarchist and members of the Irish and Northern Ireland Labour Parties, the SPNI, the (British) Independent Labour Party, and the Industrial Workers of the World. 'Non-party' includes a Quaker and volunteers designated as such or known to be of no political affiliation. (Sources: RGASPI, Moscow, International Brigades in the Spanish Republican Army, 545/6/–; Marx Memorial Library, London, International Brigades Memorial Archive; newspapers, especially the *Irish Democrat*;

O'Riordan, *Connolly Column*; and the most authoritative and comprehensive webiste on the topic, www.geocities.com/IrelandSCW/ maintained by Ciarán Crossey, Belfast International Brigades Commemorative Committee (IBCC).

The Irish were unusual too in their policy on recruitment. O'Donnell said he wanted just enough men to make a credible counterpoint to O'Duffy. His claim that hundreds had offered to fight but 'he selected only 145' was echoed by Ryan, and divers sources attest that O'Donnell, Ryan, and the CPI dissuaded them from going to Spain, arguing that they were needed at home. Tacitly accepting special treatment for the Irish, the XV International Brigade allowed Ryan to repatriate those he deemed to have done a reasonable tour of duty.[20]

Wherever the Irish in Spain formed a critical mass, they did what they could to assert their distinctive politics. The most controversial instance occurred in January 1937 when the Irish were denied battalion status for lack of numbers. In one of only two such 'mutinies' in the International Brigades, the majority left the British battalion and formed the 'James Connolly centuria' of the Abraham Lincoln battalion. The centuria commemorated Easter Week, 1916 on the Jarama front in March 1937, and organised a more official commemoration, with formal XV Brigade participation, on 12 May, the twenty-first anniversary of Connolly's execution. The gathering pledged to fight fascism internationally, and 'imperialism, native and British' at home. Just over one year later the Irish on the Ebro front marked the high point in the republican calendar with a ceremony for Wolfe Tone, founder of the United Irishmen.[21] Drawing comparisons between Spain and Ireland became a theme of 'communist republicanism'. With their strong sense of history, republicans found all sorts of connections: O'Duffy and Franco; the misuse of religion by the bishops; the nationalism of the Irish, the Basques, and the Catalans; the struggle of the landless against landlords; stories of Republican atrocities and loyalist propaganda against the insurgents in 1798; and the hysteria for 'Catholic Spain' in 1936 and 'Catholic Belgium' in 1914.[22] A similar sensibility is a feature of the satirical ballads on O'Duffy and the Christian Front by 'Somhairle MacAlastair', pseudonym of ex-IRA man Diarmuid MacGoille Phádraig.[23] Most are hilarious. 'Ballyseedy befriends Badajoz', the title linking sites of massacres of Irish and Spanish republicans, is bitter:

> O'Duffy calls his 'godly band' and leads them to the fray,
> (They murdered Liam Mellows upon Our Lady's Day),
> God help you, Spanish Connollys, if Lombard Murphy's crew
> Should blood their drunken hellhounds and send them after you…[24]

O'Donnell's *Salud!*, an account of his time in Spain at the start of the war, is almost obsessive in finding parallels. He opened the book with flashbacks to an episode in which he was caught up in a dispute over a sub-post office on Achill Island.

> I can imagine few things more exciting than to watch the days unfold against home conditions under a foreign sky; your own village is most exciting when you meet it between strange mountains…I walked into a Civil War in Achill just as I walked into one in Spain, and it was the same Civil War…A picture of Achill is a map of Spain.[25]

As the war progressed, the CPI took an increasingly republican line, even to the point of jeopardising the effort for Spain. The CPI's relations with the IRA improved when Tom Barry became chief of staff in June 1936. Though Barry banned IRA volunteers from going to Spain, the ban applied to both sides and the motivation was to keep the army focused on what he regarded as its primary purpose rather than fear of the crozier. Barry ended the IRA's proscription on CPI membership—introduced in 1933—and the party found him 'very sympathetic and helpful'.[26] Ryan resumed collaboration with the IRA, for the first time since the split in 1934. In March 1937 the CPI retired its organ, the *Worker*, in favour of the *Irish Democrat*, which was published jointly with the Republican Congress and the SPNI. The *Democrat* survived tensions over Spain: its denunciation of the POUM as 'fascists in the rear' provoked objections from the SPNI. It did not survive tensions over Ireland. The CPI complained of having to exclude IRA targeted material to accommodate the SPNI, whose membership was at once largely Protestant, anti-partition, and anti-IRA.[27] The *Irish Democrat* collapsed in December when the cash-rich SPNI withdrew its support over the paper's republican slant. Ironically, the SPNI's sizable war chest was the balance of compensation for the burning of its hall by loyalists in 1921.

The Comintern's policy was also shaped by perceived parallels between Ireland and Spain, and sought to apply to the CPI its prescriptions for the Spanish party. Augmented by the return of O'Duffy's 'fascist bravos', Comintern experts believed that the Christian Front would mount a serious challenge to Fianna Fáil in the 1937 general election, and strengthen 'developments towards fascism in Ireland…unless resolute counter-measures are taken'. To bolster Éamon de Valera's refusal to recognise the Franco regime in the face of Catholic pressure, the CPI was directed to broaden its membership, and build a new popular front that would include the rank and file of Fianna Fáil. The Comintern further considered inviting 'a small group of influential Fianna Fáil people' to Moscow, and promoting cultural and trade relations between Russia and Ireland. The CPI's election manifesto duly called, not for the replacement of Fianna Fáil, but for 'a vigorous working class and republican opposition' to make Fianna Fáil 'fight'.[28]

The general election in July 1937 was indeed a watershed for partisans of the Spanish conflict. The Fianna Fáil government survived with a reduced majority. But Fine Gael too lost ground and the Christian Front threat failed to materialise. O'Duffy's men had limped home in June, to be received with embarrassment on account of their poor military performance, and internal disputes which suggested some disillusionment with Franco and his war. On all sides, interest in Spain began to abate.

'Viva la Quince Brigada'[29]

Today, there is nothing to commemorate O'Duffy's bandera. By contrast, there are fourteen memorials to men of the Connolly Column. Plans doe more are in the pipeline. Identification with the International Brigades goes well beyond the far left. The monument in Waterford was erected on behalf of the city, and others have had the blessing of local authorities. Tributes have been paid to the Connolly Column by presidents of Ireland and lords mayor of Dublin and Belfast. In 2001, Michael O'Riordan, a veteran of the British battalion in Spain and longtime general secretary of the CPI, was invited to address the Labour Party's annual conference and hailed by the party leader as a champion of democracy in the 1930s. When Peter O'Connor, a sergeant in the Lincoln battalion, died in 1999, his death was the lead item on the flagship news bulletin of the state television channel, RTÉ 1. The same RTÉ commissioned a seven-hour television history of the state, *Seven Ages*, broadcast in 2000, which never once mentioned labour. So what is the celebration of the Connolly Column about?

The key to this question lies in the power of the Catholic Church in Ireland from the 1930s to the 1960s, and the way in which the church made anti-communism an expression of that power. The church said little on communism in the 1920s, communist public meetings attracted no hostility, and there were occasions when Fianna Fáil politicians stood on communist platforms. The coincidence of three developments in 1929–30 would change that profoundly. First, in December 1929 Josef Stalin launched a new campaign against religion in Russia. Pope Pius XI responded in 1930 by virtually excommunicating communists. Second, the Papal encyclical *Quadragesimo Anno* (1931) encouraged a specifically Catholic engagement in society and politics. Third, the centenary celebrations of

Catholic emancipation in 1929—followed by the Eucharistic Congress in Dublin in 1932—palpably demonstrated to a pleasantly surprised clergy that they were no longer of a minority church in a Protestant state, but enjoyed a virtually unchallenged status in independent Ireland. Catholic reaction emerged in early 1930, and fought a small, but growing, communist movement by creating a near totalitarian intolerance of any expression of socialism. It was clear by 1933 that the church had triumphed. While the CPI was legal, Comintern agents in Dublin complained of a 'spirit of illegality' in the party. Pat Devine reported 'serious capitulatory tendencies shown by our members in the face of [Lenten religious sermons]. On more than one occasion I had to practically force our comrades to hold [street] meetings'.[30] The climate extended to labour too—the Labour Party submitted its constitution to vetting by the hierarchy in 1938, and duly removed references found contrary to Catholic teaching—and would intensify during the height of the cold war, when any expression of socialism or leftwing internationalism was taboo.[31] Given the weakness of the left, it beggars belief that the rationale was political. Arguably, it was not theological. Plausibly, it was a means of establishing loyalty to clerical authority.

Attitudes relaxed in the 1960s. And whereas the liberalism of that decade was often justified with references to the reforming pontificate of John XXIII and the Second Vatican Council, the 1970s saw the growth of secularism, and the emergence of demands for reform of legislation on sexuality, public morality, and control of education: a socio-political force which the media labelled 'the liberal agenda'. The Catholic hierarchy won some tactical battles against 'the liberal agenda' in the 1970s, but by the mid 1980s it was patently losing the war. By the 1990s, secular liberalism was the new hegemony. The Spanish Civil War served as a reminder of how things were, and how much had changed. The Connolly Column became re-imagined as a prophetic forerunner of modern, pluralist Ireland. Just as the clergy had exploited fear of communism to demonstrate its imperium, so the left now used anti-communism to flaunt its new-found freedom, and exorcise the ghosts of its submission to clericalism. As O'Riordan observed on his invitation to address the Labour Party in 2001, it 'revers[ed] the role of that Party during the War itself'.[32]

The first Irish memorial of the Spanish Civil War was erected in 1984. Others were unveiled in 1989, 1991, 1994, 1996, 1997 and each year from 2003. The first two were in a well-worn tradition of republican remembrance, and dedicated to two republicans. Subsequent projects were led mainly by radicals of various persuasions and trade unionists, who had the advantage of access to organisation and finance. The commemorations reflected the generational gap between the 'authenticist' mentality of the Irish left in 1936 and the 'modernist' mentality of its successors. With a rooted mindset acquired from republicanism, the 'authenticists' understood Spain through the prism of Irish history. Spain was an extension of Ireland, a second front. For the 'modernists', on the other hand, Spain was (and is) an escape from the shackles of Irish history, and internationalism is a huge part of the attraction of the Connolly Column. Typically, the speeches at commemorations have focused on Catholic reaction at home, anti-fascism, and international solidarity, and represented the war as a conflict of good and evil, which drew, almost magnetically, the best men to fight the good fight. Republicanism is treated as coincidental to the background of volunteers, rather than the fundament of their politics; Spain is the focus. Belfast offers its own peculiar example of selective, 'present centred' commemoration. No fewer than four memorials appeared in the city in 2006 and 2007, commissioned by the Workers' Party, Sinn Féin, the Belfast Unemployed Resource Centre, and the IBCC. That Belfast volunteers were Catholic and Protestant makes them rather precious in a divided city, and as cross-community projects, the trades' council sponsored Unemployed Resource Centre and the IBCC emphasise the diversity of their backgrounds more than anything else. The inscription on the splendid IBCC memorial in the centre of Belfast's arts quarter uses the mincing language of Northern Ireland's peace and reconciliation industry: 'Dedicated to the people of Belfast, the island of Ireland and beyond who joined the XV International Brigade to fight Fascism in the Spanish Civil War 1936–39, and to those men and women from all traditions who supported the Spanish working people and their Republic'.[33]

What would the Connolly Column make of it all? Daiken's introduction to *Good-Bye Twilight* actually addressed the dichotomy of 'modernists' and 'authenticists'. Attributing 'almost every anomaly in recent Irish social events…*to the betrayal of the national aspirations by the Treaty of 1921* [his emphasis]', he delineated two main tendencies in Irish poetry: 'modernist' and 'traditionalist'. 'Modernism' was flight: 'traditionalism' was fight. 'Modernists' had tried to escape from Irish reality; their bourgeois aesthetic, cosmopolitanism, and 'fashionable anti-clericalism' amounted to a self-indulgent excuse for politics. However, according to Daiken, the sharpening economic crises were pushing the middle classes to the left and bringing the 'modernists' into the organic struggle never abandoned by the mainly republican 'traditionalists'.[34] Unfortunately, public opinion on the Spanish Civil War turned turtle too late for veterans to speak as they would have spoken in the 1930s. O'Donnell's edited memoir in 1974 featured a chapter on Spain without generating much interest in the subject.³⁵ When O'Riordan's *Connolly Column* appeared in 1979, it was printed in the German Democratic Republic for want of an amenable printer in Ireland. The fiftieth anniversary of Franco's revolt marked a turning point. Harry Owens, of the Post Office Workers' Union, was overwhelmed by the response to an evening of history, politics, and music which he organised in Dublin.³⁶ A stream of publications began to flow, including biographies, souvenirs, local and general histories, poems, plays and songs—Christy Moore's 'Viva la Quince Brigada' is near universally known. However, there were only five autobiographical memoirs, those by: Joe Monks (1985), Eoghan Ó Duinnín (1986), Peter O'Connor (1996), and Bob Doyle (2002 and 2006).³⁷ To the five recollections can be added oral history interviews with Frank Edwards (1980) and O'Riordan (1990), and O'Riordan's *Connolly Column* itself, which, if informative and factual, is a eulogistic CPI version of events.³⁸

These six veterans and their memoirs have a number of characteristics in common. All went into print as a contribution to radicalism, most at the prompting of younger admirers with a romantic view of Spain, which explains why the authors, apart from Ó Duinnín, were communist stalwarts to the last. Possibly because he left the party for activism 'in an individual kind of way', or possibly because he wrote in Irish, his second language, which provided a sense of distance from the text and concealment from all but the few who read it fluently, Ó Duinnín offered the most candid account, peppered with amusing anecdotes showing comrades to be more human than the unstained heroes of legend.³⁹ Monks excelled in describing front-line service, with a taut, gripping narrative. All the autobiographers leave the reader wishing they had written more, or have been challenged by what we know of the CPI since the opening of the Moscow archives. The memoirs said little on life within the party, on their authors' understanding of communism, or on the Comintern and communist politics internationally. Glossing over the fractiousness of the Irish left in the 1930s, and the sharp shifts in Comintern policy, they represented the authors in relatively bland terms as idealistic radicals, and victims of Catholic intolerance. On Spain, they dealt with military life more than politics and depicted the war as simply a struggle of democracy against fascism. All were republicans, and their 'authenticism' is evident to the trained eye, but it is also overlain with the 'modernism' of the post 1970s. Veterans who spoke at public meetings on the International Brigades from the 1980s said little on republicanism, and presented themselves as anti-fascists more than communists, ever ready to support contemporary causes, but vindicated by the restoration of liberal democracy in Spain.

Conclusion

On the eve of Ireland's accession to the European Union (EU), Lyons wrote of ex-Blueshirts and ex-IRA men reprising the Irish Civil War in 'the will-o'-the wisp of the Spanish Civil War...that had nothing to do with any of them'.[40] Recent researchers have been more impressed with how European Irish mentalities were in 1936, and how tens of thousands identified with the Catholic church, or with anti-fascism, in Spain.[41] At the same time, the Connolly Column didn't spring out of nothing. It was the product of the CPI and the Republican Congress, and the last hurrah of a socialist republicanism that can be traced to the foundation of the ITGWU by Larkin in 1909. When Labour abandoned republicanism in 1922, the communists stepped in, and the Comintern was remarkably successful in persuading a section of the IRA to adopt its *Weltanschauung*; but from the separatist tradition the 'communist republicans' acquired a rooted approach to the world. They saw the war in Spain not simply as a clash of global ideologies, but as a struggle of people like themselves—small holders, farm labourers and workers—against very familiar enemies: bishops, the army, and big landowners. Spain was the swansong of a politics throttled by clerical intolerance at home, and equally, an effort to sustain that politics in Ireland.

This 'authenticist' mentality has been lost sight of in the commemoration of the Connolly Column. The image of pre EU Ireland—a station on the highway between Europe and America, speaking the most global of languages, practicing the most catholic of religions, with a large and far flung diaspora touching almost each of its families—as introspective and isolated endures in public perceptions. And the Connolly Column, one of the great examples of Irish extroversion, has become subsumed into the myth. Not even the rehabilitation of Veterans of the Abraham Lincoln Brigade (VALB) in the United States compares with the re-discovery and lionisation of the Connolly Column. Like VALB, which has been invoked by those such as President Ronald Reagan, the Column's history has been appropriated by some implausible friends.[42] In the process, its 'communist republicanism' has been sloughed off. Its published veterans did not deny their political pedigree, but their memorialists have other values and other agendas.

Notes

1. Russian State Archive for Social and Political History (Rossiiskii Gosudartsvennyi Arkhiv Sotsial'no-Politischeskoi Istorii, RGASPI), Moscow, Memorandum on Ireland, 22 May 1937, 495/89/102–5/9.
2. J.J. Lee, *Ireland, 1912–1985: Politics and Society* (Cambridge, 1989).

3. There are two general histories of Irish communism, Mike Milotte, *Communism in Modern Ireland: The Pursuit of the Workers' Republic since 1916* (Dublin, 1984); and Emmet O'Connor, *Reds and the Green: Ireland, Russia, and the Communist Internationals, 1919–43* (Dublin, 2004). Except where stated, references to Irish communism are based on *Reds and the Green*.
4. See the British Parliamentary Paper, *Intercourse Between Bolshevism and Sinn Féin*, Cmd.1326 (1921). Another example of British propaganda is Richard Dawson, *Red Terror and Green* (London, 1920).
5. See especially T.A. Jackson, *Ireland Her Own* (London, 1947), the first Marxist general history of Ireland, and C. Desmond Greaves, *The Life and Times of James Connolly* (London, 1961), and *Liam Mellows and the Irish Revolution* (London, 1971).
6. The term was not coined until the 1970s, when it was suggested to Michael O'Riordan as a title for his eponymous history, but it has a true pedigree. The first Irish volunteers, serving in the 16th battalion, XV International Brigade, called themselves the 'Irish column', and later the 'Connolly unit'. In January 1937 a James Connolly centuria was formed in the Abraham Lincoln battalion and survived until smashed in the battle of Brunete. Michael O'Riordan, *Connolly Column: The Story of the Irishmen Who Fought in the Ranks of the International Brigades in the National-Revolutionary War of the Spanish People, 1936–1939* (Pontypool, 2005), pp.2–3 (first edn, Dublin, 1979).
7. John M. Regan, *The Irish Counter-Revolution, 1921–1936: Treaty Politics and Settlement* (Dublin, 2001), p.283.
8. Patrick F. Sheeran, *The Informer* (Cork, 2002), pp.1–12. O'Flaherty did say that the book was based on events in 'some town in Saxony', but he also claimed to be living in fear of his life in consequence of the novel. It would be quite out of keeping with his other work if O'Flaherty had not set *The Informer* in Ireland and based it on personal experience.
9. Betty Sinclair, 'A woman's fight for socialism, 1910–80', *Saothar*, 9 (1983), pp.121–32; Joe Deasy, 'The evolution of an Irish Marxist, 1941–50', *Saothar*, 13 (1988), pp.112–19; Andy Barr, 'An undiminished dream: Andy Barr, communist trade unionist', *Saothar*, 16 (1991), pp.95–111. The oral history of Sinclair is based on two lengthy taped interviews, one of which is with the CPI and the other is in the archive of the Irish Labour History Society, Dublin.
10. *Century of Endeavour* is also available in hypertext, with footnotes hotlinked to primary material, making it interactive for those wishing to engage with the author.
11. The appeal of Ernie O'Malley's memoirs, *On Another Man's Wound* (Dublin, 1936), and *The Singing Flame* (Dublin, 1978), lies partly in their exceptionality in this regard.
12. William O'Brien, *Forth the Banners Go: Reminiscences of William O'Brien as Told to Edward MacLysaght, D.Litt* (Dublin, 1969).
13. Frank Ryan, quoted in Steve Nugent, *No Coward Soul: Jack Nalty (1902–1938)* (Toronto, 2003), pp.40–1.

14. Two academic studies exist: Robert A. Stradling, *The Irish in the Spanish Civil War, 1936–1939: Crusades in Conflict* (Manchester, 1999); and Fearghal McGarry, *Irish Politics and the Spanish Civil War* (Cork, 1999).
15. McGarry, *Irish Politics and the Spanish Civil War*, pp.182–90.
16. Leslie H. Daiken (ed.), *Good-Bye, Twilight: Songs of Struggle in Ireland* (London, 1936), xviii.
17. Stradling, *The Irish and the Spanish Civil War*, p.132.
18. McGarry, *Irish Politics and the Spanish Civil War*, p.58 estimates that half of recruits to the *Connolly Column* in Ireland had been in the post Civil War IRA.
19. Communists accounted for approximately 60 per cent of French, 62 per cent of British, and 70 per cent of United States volunteers. Richard Baxell, *British Volunteers in the Spanish Civil War: The British Battalion in the International Brigades, 1936–1939* (London, 2004), pp.15, 23; Andy Durgan, 'Freedom Fighters or Comintern army? The International Brigades in Spain', *International Socialism*, 84 (autumn, 1999).
20. Michael McInerney, *Peadar O'Donnell, Irish Social Rebel* (Dublin, 1974), p.179; McGarry, *Irish Politics and the Spanish Civil War*, p.58; O'Connor, *Reds and the Green*, p.281; Uinseann McEoin, *The IRA in the Twilight Years, 1923–1948* (Dublin, 1997), p.769.
21. Frank Ryan (ed.), *The Book of the XV Brigade: Records of British, American, Canadian, and Irish Volunteers in the XV International Brigade in Spain, 1936–1938* (Pontypool, 2003), p.91 (first edn, Madrid, 1938); O'Riordan, Connolly Column, pp.2–3, 77–8, 124.
22. Comparison between Ireland and Spain was particularly marked in the *Irish Democrat*. See also the 'manifesto' of 13 International Brigaders then resident in Ireland in the *Irish Democrat*, 23 October 1937.
23. Bob Doyle, *Brigadista: An Irishman's Fight Against Fascism* (Dublin, 2006), p.143.
24. Daiken, *Good-Bye Twilight*, pp.78–9. Mellows, a prominent republican, was executed by the Free State on 8 December 1922; Lombard Murphy was the owner of the *Irish Independent*. For another example, see the poem by Mick McGinley, *Irish Democrat*, 10 April 1937.
25. Peadar O'Donnell, *Salud!: An Irishman in Spain* (London, 1937), pp.8–9.
26. O'Connor, *Reds and the Green*, pp.222–3.
27. See, for example, the attack on the IRA by Victor Halley, SPNI, *Irish Democrat*, 12 June 1937.
28. RGASPI, Proposals in connection with the CPI, 8 May 1937, 495/89/102–1/4.
29. From Christy Moore's ballad of that name.
30. RGASPI, Pat Devine to Dick [?], 10 May 1935, 495/1434–7/11.
31. Niamh Puirséil, *The Irish Labour Party, 1922–73* (Dublin, 2007), p.71.
32. O'Riordan, *Connolly Column* (2005 edn), p.4.
33. The memorials (with date of erection and dedication) are located in Achill Island (1984 to Tommy Patten); Kilgarvan, County Kerry (1989 to Michael

Lehane); Liberty Hall, Dublin (1991 to the Connolly Column); Unite (formerly the Amalgamated Transport and General Workers' Union) hall, Waterford (1994 to the 11 local International Brigaders); Unite hall Dublin (1996 to the International Brigades); Unite hall Clonmel (1997, to Amalgamated Transport and General Workers' Union solidarity with Spain, 1936–9); Coalisland, County Tyrone (2003 to Charlie Donnelly); The Mall, Waterford (2004 to the 11 local International Brigaders); Burncourt, County Tipperary (2005 to Kit Conway); the John Hewitt bar (administered by the Belfast Unemployed Resource Centre), Belfast (2006 to the International Brigades); Milltown cemetery, Belfast (2006 to 'Irish republicans who fought against fascism' in Spain); Leeson Street, Belfast (2006 to Paddy McAllister); Writers' Square, Belfast (2007, as above) ; Inistioge, County Kilkenny (2007 to the four Kilkenny International Brigaders). See Colin Williams, Bill Alexander, and John Gorman, *Memorials of the Spanish Civil War* (Stroud, 1996), pp.52–7; www.geocities.com/IrelandSCW/.
34. Daiken, *Good-Bye Twilight*, xi–xviii.
35. McInerney, *Peadar O'Donnell*, is based 'almost entirely' on interviews with O'Donnell. The chapter on Spain is fairly outline, dealing with the politics of the period.
36. Bob Doyle, *Brigadista*, pp.140–7.
37. For the extensive range of publications, varying from detailed scholarly studies to short appreciations, see www.geocities.com/IrelandSCW/. The plays include Jim Nolan, 'The Guernica Hotel' (1994), and Martin Lynch, 'Pictures of Tomorrow' (1994). Joe Monks, *With the Reds in Andalusia* (London, 1985); Eoghan Ó Duinín, *La Nina Bonita agus an Róisín Dubh: Cuimhní Cinn ar Chogadh Cathartha na Spáinne* [Nina Bonita and Róisín Dubh: Recollections of the Spanish Civil War] (Dublin, 1986); Peter O'Connor, *A Soldier of Liberty: Recollections of a Socialist and Anti-Fascist Fighter* (Dublin, 1996); and Bob Doyle, *Memorias de un Rebelde sin Pausa* (Madrid, 2002), and *Brigadista*.
38. 'Frank Edwards' in Uinseann MacEoin, *Survivors* (Dublin, 1987, first edn 1980), pp.1–20; and 'Michael O'Riordan of Cork City and the International Brigade', MacEoin, *The IRA in the Twilight Years, 1923–1948*, pp.751–66. O'Riordan has also been interviewed in newspapers and written for CPI journals on Spain.
39. The quote is from McInerney, *Peadar O'Donnell*, p.181.
40. F.S.L. Lyons, *Ireland Since the Famine* (London, 1971), p.533.
41. McGarry, *Irish Politics and the Spanish Civil War*, p.234.
42. Peter N. Carroll, *The Odyssey of the Abraham Lincoln Brigade: Americans in the Spanish Civil War* (Stanford, 1994), pp.359–80.

Comparing Revolutionary Narratives
Irish Republican self-presentation and considerations for the study of communist life-histories

Stephen Hopkins

Writing about the life histories of individuals and their experience of the 'Troubles' has been well-represented in recent published works about the conflict in Northern Ireland. The experience of Irish Republicans, revolutionary nationalists who were dedicated to the removal of British sovereignty in Northern Ireland and the creation of an all-Ireland Republic, has been central to this development. This article is based on the belief that Northern Ireland's movement towards a 'post-conflict' environment has given fresh impetus to the long-established tradition of political autobiography associated with the historical evolution of Anglo-Irish relations. Many protagonists (or ex-protagonists) of the 'Troubles', whether Irish republican/nationalist, Ulster unionist/loyalist or British, now feel the time is ripe to tell their 'stories' to a wider public, to explain their motivations, and to try and shape the historical debate over the rights and wrongs of the conflict.

In some cases, these (ex-) protagonists have used their writing to engage in self-critical reappraisal of previous commitments and actions, but perhaps it is more likely that writing in this genre and at this juncture is likely to involve a large measure of self-justification. The autobiographical design may well, in this event, represent a proxy weapon in an ongoing ideological struggle; a textual means of engaging the 'enemy' by the force of argument (as opposed to the argument of force). Rather than unvarnished 'truth-telling' with regard to the individual's role in the conflict, memoirs of this type are more likely to offer 'truths' that are 'partial, loaded and incomplete'.[1] In interpreting political autobiography in the Northern Irish context, therefore, we need to be mindful of what Roy Foster has described as 'the deliberate gap in the narrative: the momentous elision, the leap in the story'.[2] Autobiographical writing may also have a significant role to play in contemporary political discourse about how to approach 'the past' in Northern Ireland, by providing an opportunity for individual narratives to be told in their entirety, retaining their integrity, unlike for instance legal processes: 'law does not permit a single witness to tell their own coherent narrative; it chops their stories into digestible parts'.[3] This writing may also provide a symbolic, collective or communal element to the process of narrative construction, particularly when the authors are viewed as emblematic individuals. However, the lacunae or gaps that often characterise these stories make this process complex and uncertain, especially where there is still no public consensus about the essential causes of conflict. As Egerton has argued:

> with all the distortions to which this type of personal historiography is prey, the potential for honesty, accuracy and insight remains; for historians, 'truthfulness', however old-fashioned, ultimately stands as a fundamental critical concern in the evaluation of memoirs.[4]

This article starts from the premise that there is a clear absence of research that compares Irish Republican self-representation, especially through political autobiography, with that found in other self-proclaimed radical or revolutionary political movements (or erstwhile revolutionary movements), such as the communist tradition. Within the historiography of international communism, there has been, at least until recently, an 'impoverished' disregard for biography; 'historians of communism are beginning to avail themselves of the possibilities of 'life-history', even if they have scarcely explored the potential of the headier approaches to it.'[5] It has been argued that, in terms of a biographical dimension, there has been a dearth of comparative study *within* the context of the international communist movement, even although some national studies have recently begun to redress this gap.[6] It is even more clearly the case that research that compares the study of communist life-history with that found in other non-communist revolutionary political movements has been conspicuous by its absence. The following formulates some preliminary thoughts for a comparison of life-history (and specifically, autobiographical writing) within the Irish Provisional Republican movement and the West European communist movement. In particular, it does so through an analysis of Provisional Sinn Féin (PSF) President Gerry Adams's autobiographical writing, underlining some of the differences and similarities with memoirs by leaders within the West European communist movement (for instance, Harry Pollitt, General Secretary of the Communist Party of Great Britain [CPGB] and Maurice Thorez, General Secretary of the *Parti Communiste Français* [*PCF*]). Can we identify how the construction of an exemplary Provisional Republican life converges or diverges with the construction of an exemplary communist life?

The Construction of an Exemplary Irish Republican Life

'At 11.32 and 25 seconds, Gerry Adams lit his pipe. That was the signal that we were really down to business.' *An Phoblacht/Republican News* (6 November 1986)[7]

Roy Foster has argued that 'the elision of the personal and the national, the way history becomes a kind of scaled-up biography, and biography a microcosmic history, is a particularly Irish phenomenon'.[8] However, he also reminds us that there is 'a mesh of nuance, complexity and contradiction involved when the stories of nations intersect with supposedly emblematic individuals'.[9] There is a very long tradition of autobiographical writing by political leadership figures in the nationalist and republican milieu in Ireland, dating back at least to the middle of the nineteenth century.[10] In the aftermath of the crucible of guerrilla warfare and civil strife in the revolutionary period 1916–23, an earlier generation of Republicans such as Dan Breen, Ernie O'Malley and Tom Barry had developed this tradition of autobiographical writing by (ex-) protagonists of violent conflict.[11] In the recent past, one only needs to contemplate the memoirs and autobiographical fiction writing of the PSF President, Gerry Adams, or the party's erstwhile Director of Publicity, Danny Morrison, to understand the significance of this genre for the Provisional Republican movement's self-presentation.[12] At an earlier stage of the recent 'Troubles', Seán MacStiofáin, ex-Chief of Staff of the Provisional Irish Republican Army (PIRA), also published a memoir.[13]

In seeking to explore comparative elements in the Irish republican and international communist worlds of life history, it is not the intention to argue that there is any convincing ideological convergence of these movements and parties. It is probably best to understand PSF and the PIRA as a unified radical nationalist and populist movement, which may contain some socially progressive elements, but these have certainly not defined the movement's ideology. Indeed, one of the reasons for the Provisional republican movement's formation in 1969–70, out of a split in the IRA and SF, was the explicit rejection of the avowedly Marxist and communist politics associated with what became known as the 'Official' republican movement.[14] Nonetheless, until recently at any rate, the Provisionals have been an avowedly revolutionary and anti-system movement, seeking constitutional change through confrontation, often violent, with the established states in Ireland, both North and South.

However, there are arguably several similarities between the political context faced by Provisionalism in Ireland and Western communism, in terms of structure and organisation, even if not in terms of ideology. As a revolutionary movement adjusting to a non-revolutionary context, the progressive incorporation or co-option of the Provisionals into reformist and electoralist political structures, over the course of the last fifteen years or longer, and the watering down of its avowedly revolutionary method (if not the continuing aspiration towards Irish unity), has parallels with the position of west European communist parties during the post-1945 era. There has been a similar dilemma between maintaining the revolutionary 'purity' of the movement, 'pas comme les autres', and seeking to maximise its political impact in the here and now, through building a mass party, and campaigning vigorously to win positions of public influence (for example, in parliamentary elections). In Leninist parties, there was often an explicit denial that 'bourgeois parliamentarism' (winning political power through democratic electoral means) should be a primary concern for a revolutionary movement; in Irish republicanism, there was until recently a parallel denial of the legitimacy of 'partition assemblies', whether the devolved Stormont parliament in Belfast, or the Dáil in Dublin, and an even clearer rejection of the jurisdiction of the Westminster parliament in Ireland. As far as working alongside other political forces is concerned, both Irish republicans and western communists have often displayed a purely instrumental approach, viewing both competitors and potential allies with disdain. It is also clear that at least part of the organisation has been engaged in clandestine and conspiratorial (often illegal and/or violent) activity in order to further its political goals. Arguably, this 'twin track' approach to political organisation has necessitated an internal culture associated with revolutionary discipline and something akin to democratic centralism. At various junctures, the Provisionals have been accused of displaying both fascistic and communist characteristics but neither is especially persuasive, at least in ideological terms.[15]

The Provisionals have been characterised since the early 1970s by a small, self-perpetuating leadership group (including Adams and Martin McGuinness, currently SF Deputy First Minister in the Stormont parliament), and a cult of the leadership, particularly the PSF President (as the quotation that begins this section illustrates). It is worth examining further the significant parallels between the Provisional movement and communist parties, with regard to the longevity, pre-eminence and the significance attached to the origins and social background of leaders. Gerry Adams has been PSF President continuously since 1983, and before that was vice-President from 1978–1983. He has spent 35 years as one of the key strategic leaders of the Provisional movement, and has certainly become the dominant individual in his party, the 'undisputed leader', capable of inspiring awe among his supporters.[16]

Outside the movement, amongst opponents and enemies, especially during the aftermath of particularly bloody IRA actions, he has sometimes been vilified and treated as a uniquely malevolent bogey-man.[17] More recently, this position has been amended somewhat, with some outside the movement willing to fete Adams as a 'statesman' of international repute for leading the Provisionals towards an abandonment of violence.[18] However, within the Irish Republican community there are critical dissenting voices that have accused the PSF President of presiding over the neutering of the movement's revolutionary vocation.[19] There are clearly echoes here of the position held by various General Secretaries of West European Communist parties in terms of their longevity, their public standing and their internal reputation (Pollitt was GS of the CPGB for thirty years, off and on, Thorez and subsequently Georges Marchais occupied office for similar periods in the PCF, as did Palmiro Togliatti and Enrico Berlinguer in the *Partito Comunista Italiano*).

Adams was born into and became socialised within a highly politically conscious Republican family and neighbourhood milieu in west Belfast (Ballymurphy), and thus there is no conversion narrative in Adams's description of his adoption of a republican belief system in the first volume of his autobiography, *Before the Dawn*. He became a republican almost by a process of osmosis. There was no 'second birth' necessary for Adams and his republican credentials were almost incontestable from his first forays into civil rights politics in the mid-1960s. As with communist movements, Republican individuals could be ranked, and were encouraged to rank themselves, along a 'continuum of graded purity'.[20] All starting points in terms of social identity or family origins might be considered legitimate, but if a communist began life as an incontrovertible proletarian, then s/he had less work to do with regard to self-fashioning than an individual with bourgeois origins. The latter was required to demonstrate a degree of self-transformation, in order to become recognised as a 'good' communist, which the former could expect to be taken for granted.

So it was for the republican movement; an 'historic' family like the Adams/Hannaway clan (Gerry Adams senior had been jailed for attempted murder on IRA active service in 1942) had no need to wrestle with the difficult balancing act of both renouncing and embracing the 'resolutely superseded' pre-conversion self.[21] Morgan has pointed out that the 'autobiographies' of leading Western communists, because of their emblematic significance to the movement (both national and international), may be interpreted as 'a personalised form of official party history'.[22] He further argues that researchers can study these texts on the basis of three broad dimensions: anonymity, combativity and teleology, and this article utilises this schema to critically assess Adams's autobiographical self-presentation.

The Authorial Voice and Purpose

In terms of anonymity, the authorised communist 'master narrative' involves a deep-seated anti-individualism (often overlooked by those who stress the 'cult of the personality' in regard to communist leadership). The life history of the leader must be subsumed within the Party's collective ethos and values, and anything that 'might set him apart or single him out' is renounced. The leader is assimilated to the bureaucratic 'persona' of the Party, and often the first person singular (the autobiographical 'I') is eschewed for the plural.[23] Jochen Hellbeck has also investigated Soviet subjectivity in the Stalinist period, through a study of individuals' diaries, and he asks 'what is meant by writing the word *I* in an age of a larger *We*'.[24] This formulation has echoes of Victor Serge's fictional (but partly autobiographical) recreation of the same period, in his *The Case of Comrade Tulayev* (1948). In the novel, Serge has the character of Makeyev (a Tsarist soldier who becomes a Bolshevik during the civil war, and rises rapidly through the party hierarchy, becoming an alternate member of the communist party central committee in 1925) reflect upon the blurred nature of his individual self-identity, and his relationship with the collectivity of the Party:

> 'All is ours!' he said, sincerely, at public meetings of the Railwaymen's Club, and he could easily have substituted 'All is mine,' since he was only vaguely aware where 'I' ended and 'we' began. (The 'I' belongs to the Party, the 'I' is of value only inasmuch as, through the Party, it incarnates the new collectivity; yet, since it incarnates it powerfully and consciously, the 'I', in the name of the 'we', possesses the world.)[25]

The apogee of this approach can be seen in the production process; there is evidence from the German Democratic Republic of memoir writing being undertaken by Party committee (there was a Memoir Section of the Institute of Marxism-Leninism in East Berlin).[26] In the case of Thorez's *Fils du Peuple* (first published in 1937, but regularly republished in amended form, to bring the text into line with current political orthodoxy, up until 1960) the narrative was ghost-written by Jean Fréville and subsequently edited by senior

PCF ideologists. It has been described as a 'socialist realist' autobiography.[27] Morgan argues that in this schema 'the mildest deprecation of self or party' was taboo, and 'not human frailty or temptation but a steely self-control was expected'.[28]

In this case, modern Irish republicanism may be somewhat diverse. Gerry Adams, for instance, was already a writer of some repute (in the genres of local history and autobiographical fiction), before he published his two volumes of political autobiography so far, *Before the Dawn: An Autobiography* (1996) and *Hope and History: Making Peace in Ireland* (2003). There is no doubt that Adams himself is the authentic author of his narratives, although he does regularly recognise the aid of some prominent and trusted confidants (such as Richard McAuley, PSF press officer/spin doctor, and Steve MacDonogh, his editor/publisher at Brandon/Mount Eagle). Furthermore, Adams employs a subtle device, utilising self-deprecation (or even self-mockery) and acknowledgement of personal frailties as a badge of authenticity, introducing a note of bathos into his writing. This studied folksiness or affected simplicity is supposed to convey humility; he may not be a paragon of revolutionary virtue, and perhaps he suffers from similar faults to the rank-and-file grassroots republicans. The purpose of this is to establish Adams as a grounded 'man of the people' who understands and even shares their foibles, but also their dreams. In this regard, Adams's narrative shares many of the characteristics that have been associated with Harry Pollitt's *Serving My Time* (1940), 'a narrative conforming to the wider conventions of British labour autobiography at least as much as to the special requirements of a communist party life'.[29] In Adams's case, we can speculate that this distinctive approach may, in part, reflect a less deferential era, a time when any attempt to hold up the leader as an wholly virtuous incarnation of all that is 'pure' in the movement is no longer credible, even in authoritarian parties.

For instance, Adams recalls that in the initial stages of the inter-party talks process leading up to the Good Friday Agreement, when unionists were deeply distrustful of republican intentions, 'most of my best conversations with unionists were in the toilets. It was just small talk.'[30] The effect sought here is to convey Adams's willingness to fraternise with the 'enemy', his non-dogmatic openness to dialogue, in contrast to the intransigence of Ulster Unionist leader, David Trimble. Interestingly, there are distinct echoes here of the unorthodox approach to communist memoir adopted by Harry Pollitt, who also jokingly recalled fraternising with police officers and industrialists. No doubt, some of these anecdotal interventions are genuinely humorous but that ought not to deflect us from their determinedly political purpose.³¹ Foster notes Adams's professed enjoyment of P. G. Wodehouse's writing; he argues that this 'is inevitably linked with a carefully calculated joke that, like Jeeves, he has to go around clearing up the mess left behind by Englishmen'.³²

It is also worth saying something about fact and fiction in Adams's writing. His two volumes of memoir were preceded by *Cage Eleven* (1990), a book based on his 'Brownie' articles written while he was an internee and then a convicted prisoner (after a failed escape attempt), and published in *Republican News* between 1975 and 1977. Although Adams gives the real names of some of his fellow internees in the book's introduction, he later claims that 'the main characters are fictional, but they and their escapades are my way of representing life as it was in Long Kesh'.³³ Steve MacDonogh characterises his literary development (at least before his memoirs were published) as a gradual move away from factual writing towards fiction. Introducing Adams's *Selected Writings* (1994), he explains that while *Falls Memories: A Belfast Life* (1982), a local history of a Catholic nationalist area of Belfast, has 'qualities of fiction', and Cage Eleven 'hover[s] between fact and fiction', *The Street and Other Stories* (1992) is 'more decidedly fictional'.³⁴

In *Before the Dawn*, however, Adams's propensity to blur the margins between fact and fiction provoked controversy when he 'tried to capture in a short story something of the harsh reality of the campaign waged by the IRA against Britain's armed forces as they patrolled the streets of my home town' in the early 1970s.³⁵ Although this 'story', which recounts the internal moral questioning of an PIRA sniper before he shoots a member of a British army patrol, is written in italics, it is not explicitly presented purely as fiction, the product only of imagination rather than experience. Fintan O'Toole criticised the evasiveness of Adams's narrative style, adding: 'it is striking in itself that the IRA campaign on the streets of Belfast is not represented by bombs tearing civilians apart in restaurants, by children blown up on their way into the Falls Road baths or by "informers" having nail-studded clubs aimed at their flesh'.³⁶ There was, of course, a political rationale behind this approach; Adams could only present such details in 'fictional' form because of his steadfast denial that he has ever been a member of the PIRA, despite the incredulity and derision of critics. Nevertheless, the strength of the critical reaction that greeted this aspect of his autobiographical style seems to have had an impact; certainly, no similar episode appears in *Hope and History*.

Conveying the Struggle: An Ambiguous Strategy

Although Gerry Adams is willing to use personal anecdotes to supplement and further his political purpose, nevertheless this makes any perceived dissimulation on his part more damaging. Of course, Adams is by no means alone in utilising what Aughey has described as 'the art of political lying'; as McIntyre has pointed out, the idea of the 'revolutionary lie' has been used by many organisations that accept the logic of the ends justifying the means.[37] Adams wants to identify himself in *Before the Dawn* with the heroic communal sacrifice and struggle of the republican community and its 'army', the PIRA, but this identification inevitably leads him into an ambivalent position as far as the actual campaign of violence is concerned. His position is complicated by his strategic purpose at the time of publication (1996): first, he wanted to distance the political 'wing' of the Provisional movement from the military, arguing against all the evidence that they are in fact entirely separate organisations; Adams's oft-repeated argument is that the former deserved to be involved in all-party talks because of its electoral mandate alone. One way to achieve this was for Adams to deny ever having played a prominent role in the PIRA, or indeed having been a member at all; second, with the benefit of hindsight, we can speculate that he wished to prepare the ground for the definitive abandonment of armed struggle, but he could not state this openly, for fear of provoking a serious split in the movement.

His credibility on this issue has been undermined by a succession of biographers and commentators, and there is virtual unanimity amongst academic researchers: 'between April/May 1971 and March 1972 Gerry Adams was OC of the Provisionals' 2nd Battalion in Belfast; in the latter year he became Adjutant for the Belfast Brigade as a whole; by the time of his arrest on 19 July 1973 he had become OC of the entire Belfast Brigade...Adams was released from prison in 1977 and in the same year became an Army Council member, a position which he was to hold for a long time'.[38] Most accounts also agree that Adams was, for a short period at the end of 1977 until February 1978, the PIRA's Chief of Staff.[39] In fact it is harder than ever to take seriously Adams's claims, given Martin McGuinness's recent admission that he was a significant PIRA commander in Derry at the time of Bloody Sunday in 1972, an admission that perhaps heralds a change of heart at the apex of the organisation. Nevertheless, as O'Toole has observed, *Before the Dawn* 'almost entirely glossed over' Adams's IRA career, a view endorsed by Foster, who claims that he is 'unnecessarily coy' about the IRA and likens his memoir to 'a biography of Field Marshal Montgomery that leaves out the British Army'.[40] The political subtext was clear to all, however. The context of the developing peace process, and the perceived requirement to maintain Adams's position as the Provisionals' unchallenged leader, capable of delivering a PIRA ceasefire and committing (at least the vast bulk of) the movement to this new strategy, meant that 'these incredible assertions were allowed to pass with no more than mild expressions of skepticism'.[41] If Adams was to be accepted locally and internationally as a genuine agent of peace *and* compromise, then it suited the purposes of governments in London, Dublin and Washington, as well as republicans and even pro-Agreement unionists, to collude in this necessary fiction.

However, as O'Toole notes, 'the danger has always been that the tacit agreement to ignore the IRA past of the SF leader would encourage a larger and more profound act of denial. If Adams did not have to account for his involvement with the IRA, then perhaps the IRA itself could remain unaccountable.'[42] More than ten years after the signing of the Agreement, this issue of accountability for past actions remains central to Northern Ireland's political future. Adams must have been more aware than most of the likely reaction to his address at the PSF-sponsored March for Truth Rally (August 2007), in which he called for full disclosure of the British state's role in 'violence and collusion' with loyalist paramilitary 'death squads' during the Troubles. Entirely predictably, Adams was roundly condemned from many quarters for his apparent hypocrisy; a senior political source at Stormont was quoted as saying, 'It's a case of "be careful what you wish for" because the whole truth and nothing but the truth would have far more serious consequences for Adams and co. than anyone else'.[43] Families and victims of alleged state collusion, who may well have legitimate grievances that deserve to be investigated impartially, must also surely recognise that recruiting Gerry Adams to publicise their case will inevitably lead to accusations that they are willing pawns in a party political game, where the 'truth' is merely harnessed to party calculation at any given moment.

The motifs of communal endurance and resistance are repeated at virtually every turn in Adams's memoirs, and he consciously adopts an omniscient stance, seeking to symbolise and embody this spirit. Adams readily eulogises the republican base's stubborn refusal to buckle under enormous pressure, despite the tough conditions that it had to endure whilst sustaining the guerrilla conflict. However, one of the consequences of prosecuting the war, according to Adams, is that it helped to create an under-developed political consciousness within the movement's heartlands. The implication, though not explicit, is that only he (and a few other perspicacious members of the leadership coterie) can be aware of the broader context within which the Provisionals' heroic resistance was played out, and only this hand-picked close-knit group can fully appreciate the newly changed political circumstances. Ordinary activists and foot soldiers are conceived as incapable of this sort of deeper strategic and political thinking, and are therefore almost completely reliant on the wisdom and far-sightedness of their leaders. Again, the parallels with communist parties, and their intolerance of internal questioning and dissent, are strikingly clear. This may have been convincing within the Provisional movement whilst PSF were making steady electoral progress, but as a result of more recent setbacks (particularly in the general election in the Republic of Ireland in 2007) increasingly questions are being asked, and perhaps Adams's hitherto unchallengeable position will be less secure.

Finally, in this section, what is clear is that Adams's 'most passionate commitment is to the narrow world of West Belfast, a self-justifying and tightly-knit community later replicated in the republican wing of internment prison'.[44] Adams's story is couched in localised terms, partly due to his desire during the mid-1990s to confirm the republican heartlands in their belief that the 'revolutionary struggle' had not been defeated, despite the PIRA ceasefire, and that all of the sacrifices had been worthwhile. It also makes his self-appointed task of subsuming his personal story into the heroic collective 'resistance' of the republican community much easier. Indeed, as Foster has argued, Adams 'is determined to see things purely in the perspective framed by his mother's back window', although this localism is, of course, a conscious political decision, masking a much broader strategic, and cunning, intent.[45] In contrast to this disingenuously parochial image, he 'enjoys' massive worldwide exposure: in marketing terms, 'as an Irish product, Gerry Adams has name recognition rivalling Guinness or Waterford Glass'.[46] He purports, moreover, to be a 'very shy person', explaining: 'I find other people are much more relaxed in dealing with public events. I mean, I wouldn't be running about to banquets or balls or fancy suppers. It's nothing to those who lost their lives…or lost loved ones, but I think the loss of anonymity is a big thing'.[47] Adams's target audience in Ireland and (especially, the USA) is again invited to see him as a grounded politician who understands them and their community; in short, as a 'man of the people'.

The Teleological Imperative: United Ireland

If Adams's autobiographical writing is guarded and opaque, this is explicable in terms of his perception of the *political* imperatives of the republican movement at that particular juncture, though this does not of itself render such an approach justifiable to a wider readership. Foster acknowledges that 'since the Adams story is a small part of the story of modern Ireland, so the fact that it supplies—yet again—a narrative of evasions is only appropriate'.[48] O'Toole notes that 'political autobiographies should be written when the hurly-burly's done. They should tell a story whose ending is known, reflect on something that has actually been achieved.'[49] There is a clear parallel here with the communist autobiographies we have mentioned (Pollitt's was published when he was aged fifty, yet he still had another sixteen years to serve as CPGB leader; Thorez's was first published when he was only thirty-seven, and still had twenty-five years to come at the apex of the PCF). But, the end of Adams's story remains unpredictable (he was only forty-eight when his first volume of memoir came out), because as he recognises in the foreword to *Before the Dawn*:

> I am also conscious that the elements of conflict remain today and retain their potency. For this reason I must write nothing which would place in jeopardy the liberties or the lives of others, so I am necessarily constrained. It is probably an invariable rule that the participants in any conflict cannot tell the entire story until some time after that conflict is fully resolved.[50]

These words were written in February 1996 when, with the end of the IRA's ceasefire at Canary Wharf, it was the Provisionals' actions rather than Adams's text that was taking lives, and not merely jeopardising them. Even today, Adams would no doubt take the view that the conflict has yet to be 'fully resolved'. Indeed it is arguable that when Adams talks of the conflict requiring complete resolution before he could tell 'the entire story', the only circumstance that would satisfy his criterion is the creation of a united Ireland, or at least PSF in government across the island. Again, just as there is a teleological core at the heart of Adams's thinking, the parallel with the communist view of the necessary conditions for the ending of class conflict is striking.

Despite the absence of discernible movement towards a united Ireland, in 2003 Adams brought out a second volume of autobiography.[51] However, *Hope and History: Making Peace in Ireland*, came no closer to offering a 'real and fully truthful autobiography'.[52] Rather, it presented the author's version of the process leading up to the successful negotiation of the Agreement in April 1998, and while there is a perfunctory final chapter outlining some of the problems it has encountered in subsequent years, Adams has conceded (again) that the narrative remains unfinished: 'there is a natural third book… but apart from noting that in my head, I have no plans, notions, ambitions to even think about writing it at the moment'.[53] Moreover, he insists that since the 'story' of the peace process is 'still unfolding, still sensitive, still fragile…it is not my business to offer an objective account of events or to see through someone else's eyes. Nor is it my responsibility to document these events. My intention is to tell a story. It is my story. My truth. My reality.'[54] The rationale for publication at this particular time, therefore, seems to be that 'a happy ending'—the signing of the Agreement—is 'more important than a tell-all story'.

Once more, Adams also conflates his 'personal journey' with the communal story. The peace process in his eyes is presented as a morality tale, where selfless nationalists—notably John Hume of the SDLP and Catholic clerics such as Fr Alec Reid—and republicans consistently urge the British government and the unionist parties to address 'the underlying causes of conflict', as if these are self-evident, uncomplicated and uncontested. He places enormous emphasis upon his dialogue with Hume and the quest for pan-nationalist unity in the early 1990s, and the need to press the Dublin and Washington administrations to adopt the 'Irish peace initiative', with no apparent recognition that, without a balancing input from the Westminster government, no serious negotiation with *any section* of unionism would be feasible. Indeed, the unionists as an autonomous force hardly figure at all in Adams's narrative. Interestingly, his later overtures to unionism are revealed as merely a rhetorical device:

> the mess within unionism is inherently part of any process of change. Unionism *at its best* is quite a conservative, reactionary philosophy….I've been reading recently Faulkner's memoirs, different bits and pieces of writings by unionist leaders…and you'd almost think that some of the senior British officials, some of the NIO people, are using a script written in the 1920s or 1970s.[55]

But, doesn't Adams's own presentation of his political thought imply that his own 'script' remains fundamentally unaltered? From this perspective, the 1993 Downing Street Declaration is seen as no more than 'a significant development', though an alternative reading would suggest that without it there would have been no potential for progress towards genuinely inclusive talks. Republicans had to be provided with an alternative to 'armed struggle' before peace was possible, says Adams, but the unanswered question remains: what happens if the republican movement maintains its evolution into a party 'like all the others', if the military wing is entirely dismantled, and the 'struggle' is pursued solely through the democratic process, but the outcome is not Irish unity, at least not any time soon? The teleology inherent in Adams's narrative means that he cannot entertain such an outcome; a 'proper' democracy, in his view, is defined as leading inexorably to a sovereign, united Republic.[56] Even today, there is no adequate answer to this question, but it is becoming starker for many ordinary Republicans. Perhaps for the first time, Adams's self-proclaimed revolutionary vocation is being subjected to close scrutiny, and not just by 'dissidents', but also by hitherto devoted supporters. Anthony McIntyre, commenting on recent criticism of Adams in the usually compliant *Andersonstown News*, has argued that Adams 'now stands increasingly isolated as the sole remaining dinosaur of Northern Irish politics…an antediluvian figure from the 1980s.'[57]

Conclusion

We can tentatively draw a number of conclusions from this comparison of the construction of exemplary communist and republican lives: both share a rejection of the false dichotomy that is often posited between individual and societal processes of remembering, and both construct narratives that identify the individual leader as emblematic of the wider political community. In both cases, we can speculate about the impact that a loss of revolutionary vocation or at least of self-confidence has had on the respective autobiographical projects. Paradoxically, despite the shared teleological vision, both of these movements were progressively integrated into the political systems they were ostensibly committed to overthrowing. Perhaps the autobiographical design is meant to make sense of this development for the rank-and-file. From this perspective, they are pragmatic attempts to conscript the past in the service of the movement's present strategy, which is unfolding in a non-revolutionary context.

Adams's approach to political autobiography, therefore, is to echo, through the mask of supposedly personal testimony, the officially-endorsed and internally-validated version of 'party' history, and to use this testimony in the service of his contemporary goals. In this way, autobiographical reflection is harnessed to the yoke of political expediency. If the 'revolutionary movement' progressively loses its revolutionary vocation, then what is left? For a leader like Adams, just as for communist leaders like Georges Marchais, the answer is internal power. To the question posed by Sharrock and Devenport in the title of their unauthorised biography of Adams: *Man of War or Man of Peace?* we can juxtapose McIntyre's view that Adams should be understood, above all, as a Man of Power![58]

Notes

1. F. Meredith, 'Rounded, intelligent, articulate, human and murderous', *Fortnight*, 412 (2003), p.8.
2. R. Foster, *The Irish Story: Telling Tales and Making it up in Ireland* (London, 2002), p.3.
3. A. Hegarty, 'Truth, justice and reconciliation? The problems with truth processes', *Global Review of Ethnopolitics*, 2 (2002), p.100.
4. G. Egerton (ed.), *Political Memoir: Essays on the Politics of Memory* (London, 1994), p.348.
5. Preface in J. McIlroy, K. Morgan, A. Campbell (eds), *Party People, Communist Lives: Explorations in Biography* (London, 2001), p.5.
6. In the British context, see *inter alia*, K. Morgan, G. Cohen, A. Flinn, *Communists and British Society 1920–1991* (London, 2007). For an international perspective, though not strictly a comparative approach, see Morgan, Cohen, Flinn (eds), *Agents of the Revolution: New Biographical Approaches to the History of International Communism in the Age of Lenin and Stalin* (Bern, Switzerland, 2005).
7. Cited in Eoin O'Malley, 'Populist Nationalists: Sinn Féin and Redefining the "Radical Right"', Paper presented to the *Elections, Public Opinion and Parties* conference, Nottingham, 1996, p.14.
8. Foster, *The Irish Story*, p.xi.
9. Foster, *The Irish Story*, p.xvii.
10. For example, see J. Mitchel, *Jail Journal* (Poole, 1996 [1854]); J. Denvir, *Life Story of an Old Rebel* (Shannon, 1972 [1910]).
11. D. Breen, *My Fight for Irish Freedom* (Dublin, 1989 [1924]); Ernie O'Malley, *On Another Man's Wound* (Dublin, 1979 [1936]) and *The Singing Flame* (Dublin, 1978); T. Barry, *Guerrilla Days in Ireland* (Dublin, 1989 [1949]).
12. See inter alia by G. Adams, *Cage Eleven* (Dingle, 1990); *Falls Memories: A Belfast Life* (Dingle, 1982); *Selected Writings* (Dingle, 1994); *Before the Dawn: An Autobiography* (London, 1996); *Hope and History: Making Peace in Ireland* (Dingle/London, 2003); *The New Ireland: A Vision for the Future* (Dingle/London, 2005); *An Irish Eye* (Dingle/London, 2007); D. Morrison, *Then the Walls Came Down: A Prison Journal* (Cork/Dublin, 1999); *All the Dead Voices* (Cork/Dublin, 2002).
13. S. MacStiofáin, *Memoirs of a Revolutionary* (Edinburgh, 1975).
14. For further information on the split in the republican movement in 1969–70, see R. English, *Armed Struggle: A History of the IRA* (London, 2003), pp.81–147; H. Patterson, *The Politics of Illusion: A Political History of the IRA* (London, 1997), pp.96–139. On the Officials, see S. Swan, *Official Irish Republicanism, 1962–1972* (2007) and R. Dunphy and S. Hopkins, 'The Organisational and Political Evolution of the Workers' Party of Ireland', *Journal of Communist Studies*, Vol.8, No.3 (1992).
15. In 1994, the British ambassador to the United States, Sir Robin Renwick, specifically compared Gerry Adams with Joseph Goebbels (*New Statesman*, 21 March 2005). John Bruton, Fine Gael prime minister in the Republic of

Ireland in the mid-1990s, explicitly compared the Provisional movement with the Nazi party (D. Sharrock and M. Devenport, *Man of War, Man of Peace? The Unauthorised Biography of Gerry Adams* [London, 1997], pp.416–17). An unnamed senior British official more recently described the PSF approach to internal discipline as 'Stalinist' (*Guardian*, 13 March 2007).
16. A. Maillot, *New Sinn Féin: Irish Republicanism in the Twenty-first Century* (London, 2005), p.98.
17. After Adams helped carry the coffin of the IRA man Thomas Begley, who had, in October 1993, blown himself up along with nine people in a fish shop on the strongly loyalist Shankill Road in West Belfast, the British press reacted furiously: 'Gerry Adams: the two most disgusting words in the English language' said the *Sun* in its editorial (Sharrock and Devenport, *Man of War, Man of Peace?* p.310).
18. Nancy Soderberg, the Clinton administration's leading official on Northern Irish policy during the early 1990s peace process, invoked the name of Nelson Mandela when discussing the importance of Adams to the process (*New Statesman*, 21 March 2005). A decade later, after the terrorist attacks of 11 September 2001, the allegations of IRA training FARC rebels in Colombia, and Adams's visit to Havana to acknowledge the support of the Cuban administration for Irish republicanism, mainstream US opinion was much less enamoured; the *New York Post* headlined an article about Adams 'Osama's soul brother' (10 November 2002).
19. Aside from the relatively small organised republican alternatives to the Provisional movement, in the shape of *Republican* Sinn Féin/Continuity IRA and the 32 County Sovereignty movement/Real IRA, there have been several non-aligned republicans who have been a constant thorn in the side for Adams and the PSF leadership. Perhaps the best known is Anthony McIntyre, who ran an influential website, *The Blanket* that regularly castigated the PSF President, and the alleged centralism and censorship employed by the Provisionals.
20. I. Halfin, *Terror in my Soul: Communist Autobiographies on Trial* (Cambridge, MA, 2003), p.27.
21. Sharrock and Devenport, *Man of War, Man of Peace?* pp.5–35; Halfin, *Terror in my Soul*, p.50. For the importance of the 'family' as a site of communist socialisation, see P. Cohen, *Children of the Revolution: Communist Childhood in Cold War Britain* (London, 1997), and R. Samuel, *The Lost World of British Communism* (London, 2006), pp.59–76.
22. Morgan, 'An Exemplary Communist Life? Harry Pollitt's *Serving My Time* in comparative perspective', in J. Gottlieb and R. Toye (eds), *Making Reputations: Power, Persuasion and the Individual in Modern British Politics* (London, 2005), p.56; C. Guiat, *The French and Italian Communist Parties: Comrades and Culture* (London, 2003), p.58.
23. S. Sirot, *Maurice Thorez* (Paris, 2000), p.28 cited in Morgan, 'Exemplary Life', p.3.
24. J. Hellbeck, *Revolution on my Mind: Writing a Diary under Stalin* (Cambridge, MA, 2006), p.xi (Italics in original).

25. V. Serge (*pseud.*), *The Case of Comrade Tulayev* (New York, 2004), p.101. For a fuller discussion see Hopkins, 'Review Essay: The Soviet Politics of the Self', *Labour History Review*, 73 (2008), pp.336–47. In the French context, see J. Gaffney, *The French Left and the Fifth Republic: the discourses of communism and socialism in contemporary France* (London, 1989).
26. For further details see C. Epstein, *The Last Revolutionaries: German Communists and their Century* (Cambridge, MA, 2003); C. Epstein, 'The Production of "Official Memory" in East Germany: Old Communists and the Dilemmas of Memoir-Writing', *Central European History*, 32 (1999), p.185.
27. On Thorez's *Fils du peuple* see C. Pennetier and B. Pudal, 'Stalinisme, culte ouvrier et culte des dirigeants', in M. Dreyfus et al. (eds), *Le Siècle des Communismes* (Paris, 2004), pp.553–63. Also Morgan, 'Exemplary Life' and Pennetier and Pudal, 'Les Autobiographies des "fils du people": de l'autobiographie édifiante à l'autobiographie auto-analytique', in Pennetier and Pudal (eds), *Autobiographies, autocritiques, aveux dans le monde communiste* (Paris, 2002).
28. Morgan, 'Parts of People and Communist Lives', in J. McIlroy, K. Morgan, A. Campbell (eds), *Party People, Communist Lives: Explorations in Biography* (London, 2001), p.13.
29. Morgan, 'Exemplary Life', pp.59–60.
30. Adams, *Hope and History*, p.311.
31. J. Harkin, 'Unifying Force' (*Guardian*, 17 December 2005) noted of his interview with Adams that his sense of humour is 'drier than dust.' Adams himself (*Guardian*, 24 August 2007) recently wrote a comic piece about the attention he receives from security personnel at airports during his frequent travels to the US: 'The man behind the desk was friendly. "You must be Irish," he said. "You look like that guy, Adams." "I know," I said. "He's always getting me into trouble."'
32. Foster, 'Adams' Original Sin', *Financial Times Magazine*, 23 October 2004.
33. Adams, *Cage Eleven*, p.14.
34. S. MacDonogh, 'Introduction', in G. Adams, *Selected Writings* (Dingle, 1994), pp.x–xii.
35. Adams, *Before the Dawn*, p.168.
36. F. O'Toole, 'The Premature Life of Gerry Adams', *Irish Times*, 28 September 1996.
37. A. Aughey, 'The Art and Effect of Political Lying in Northern Ireland', *Irish Political Studies*, 17 (2002), pp.7–11; A. McIntyre, 'The Battle against Truth', *The Blanket*, 19 August 2007.
38. R. English, *Armed Struggle*, p.110. See also Sharrock and Devenport, *Man of War, Man of Peace?* p.116; C. Keena, *Gerry Adams: A Biography* (Dublin/Cork, 1990), pp.53, 72–3, 79; K. Kelley, *The Longest War: Northern Ireland and the IRA* (Dingle, 1983), p.128; C. de Baróid, *Ballymurphy and the Irish War* (London, 2000 rev. edn), p.33; M.L.R. Smith, *Fighting for Ireland? The Military Strategy of the Irish Republican Movement* (London, 1995), p.145; P. Taylor, *Provos: The IRA and Sinn Féin* (London, 1997), pp.201–2.

39. E. Moloney, *A Secret History of the IRA* (London, 2002), pp.172–3.
40. F. O'Toole, 'The Taming of a Terrorist', *New York Review*, 27 February 2003, p.14; R. Foster, *The Irish Story*, pp.177–8. McIntyre chose a metaphor from closer to home when he compared Adams's omission of his IRA career as akin to George Best telling his life-story but failing to mention that he had played for Manchester United. Cited in R. Dudley Edwards, 'Gerry the Liar', *Spectator*, 27 July 2002; in another metaphor, Roy Foster argued that it was about as credible as Paul McCartney denying his past membership of the Beatles, *Financial Times Magazine*, 23 October 2005.
41. O'Toole, 'The Taming of a Terrorist', p.14.
42. O'Toole, 'The Taming of a Terrorist', p.14.
43. 'Victims ask Adams: where is our truth?', *Newsletter*, 11 August 2007. See also B. Feeney, 'Adams calls for truth but keeps past secret', *Irish News*, 16 August 2007; *An Phoblacht*, 16 August 2007.
44. Foster, *The Irish Story*, p.176.
45. Foster, *The Irish Story*, p.177.
46. *Irish Independent*, 30 September 2003.
47. C. Thornton, 'Vintage Adams: His life in books', *Belfast Telegraph*, 29 September 2003.
48. Foster, *The Irish Story*, p.181.
49. O'Toole, 'The Premature Life of Gerry Adams'.
50. Adams, *Before the Dawn*, Foreword, p.2.
51. D. Sharrock, 'Adams signs £400,000 deal for new book', *Daily Telegraph*, 10 October 2001.
52. O'Toole, 'The Premature Life of Gerry Adams'. Suzanne Breen argues that in his 'studied attempt to exhibit emotion and sincerity' Adams veers between 'statesmanlike' and 'folksy' throughout ('The Many Tales of Gerry Adams', *News Letter*, 2 October 2003).
53. Thornton, 'Vintage Adams: His life in books', *Belfast Telegraph*, 29 September 2003.
54. Adams, *Hope and History*, p.2.
55. Adams cited in P. Leahy, 'Trimble knows the old days are over', *Sunday Business Post*, 28 September 2003. Emphasis added.
56. See the extensive interview with Adams conducted by Nick Stadlen (*Guardian*, 12 September 2007). Asked whether the IRA's armed struggle was justified, given what was on offer at Sunningdale in 1973, and what republicans settled for in the 1998 Agreement, Adams replied, 'Well, you can only—at the risk of scaring the unionist horses—you can only make that judgment at the end, and the end in my view will be a united Ireland.'
57. A. McIntyre, 'And Goodbye Adams?' *Parliamentary Brief*, April 2008. See also M. O'Doherty, 'Could Gerry Adams be living on borrowed time?' *Belfast Telegraph*, 16 May 2008.
58. McIntyre, 'Gerry Adams: Man of War and Man of Peace?' Lecture delivered at Manchester Metropolitan University, 28 April 2004.

Perspectives

Berlinguer's 'Democratic Alternative'
U-turn or continuity?
Giuseppe Vatalaro

Enrico Berlinguer was the General Secretary of the Italian Communist Party (PCI) from 1972 until his death in 1984. From 1973 and until the end of the decade, Berlinguer focused the party's strategy on what he defined as the 'historic compromise', a proposed governmental alliance between the PCI and the Christian Democratic Party (DC), which had been a consistent feature of Italian Government from the first post-war general election in 1948. Such an alliance was meant to give Italy the political stability that was necessary for the country to overcome a period of economic crisis and social turmoil. Berlinguer insisted that the PCI wanted to govern together with and not against the DC, even in the event of the communists gaining 50 per cent plus one of the votes. In spite of the apparent social democratic connotation of this strategy, the General Secretary constantly maintained that the 'historic compromise' was a fundamental step in the party's hegemonic struggle for the transition of Italy to socialism. Accordingly, a few years later, Berlinguer augmented the communist programme with an 'austerity policy', calling for economic measures promoting solidarity not only amongst the different social classes in Italy, but also between the richest and the poorest parts of the world, thus facilitating the introduction of 'elements of Socialism' within a capitalist framework.

At the end of the 1970s and the beginning of the 1980s Berlinguer's leadership was characterised by a change of policy from the 'historic compromise' to the 'democratic alternative', which from the mid 1980s became the 'programmatic alternative'. Scholarship tends to assess Berlinguer's new strategy, and more generally the history of the party in the 1980s—ending, in 1991, two years after the collapse of the Berlin Wall, with the dismantling of the PCI to form the Democratic Party of the Left, and entry into the Socialist International—from two different viewpoints. These are based on two opposing interpretations of the nature of the PCI's communist identity. An unsympathetic perspective generally supports an 'Iron Link' view, conceiving of the party's communist identity as rooted in its historical ties to Stalinist authoritarianism. Within this interpretative framework, the 'democratic alternative' and the last decade of the PCI are generally seen as dominated by the failings of communist leadership until the collapse of the Berlin Wall freed the party's identity from its links to the Soviet Union.[1] On the other hand, more sympathetic commentators, generally holding an 'evolutionary' view of the PCI's development, see the 1980s as a period in which the process of the PCI's transformation—which is thought to have characterised the entire history of the party—and the eventual full acceptance of the pluralist values of liberal Western democracy were substantially accelerated; this was especially the case following an increasing erosion within the party of the principles of democratic centralism, thus allowing an extension of internal democracy and the party's complete laicisation.[2]

Both interpretations, though from different perspectives, tend to see the 'democratic alternative', and the changes that the PCI underwent throughout the 1980s, within a continuum in the party's history, rather than as a watershed introducing a fundamental break in the party's identity. Even those scholars who reconstruct the transformation of the party into the new PDS in terms of discontinuity rather than continuity are inclined to argue that the break with the past took place only at the very end of the PCI's history in 1991.[3] Thus, the 'Iron-Link' perspective sees the continuity between the party's previous history and that of the 1980s in a communist identity too anchored to the Soviet Union. On the other hand from the 'evolutionary' standpoint the metamorphosis of the PCI is seen as an unbroken trajectory, from the 1944 Salerno u-turn—where Togliatti put an end to calls for armed revolution and committed the PCI to participation in government together with the other democratic forces—to the party's transformation into the PDS, or at least until the party's XVIII Congress in 1989. Such a trajectory, it is generally maintained within this perspective, was characterised by the growing dominance of the PCI's reformist soul over its revolutionary spirit.[4] Thus, whereas the more critical perspective concludes that the 1980s can be considered '*residuali*' ('residual') in the party's history,[5] the more sympathetic scholarship tends to see this period as that of the definitive transformation of the party into a modern social-democratic force of the left, facilitated by the dismantling of democratic centralism, through which 'the long-festering division between left and right' had until then been prevented 'from fully and publicly entrenching their opposing viewpoints'.[6]

Vassilis Fouskas's reconstruction of the transformation of the PCI into the PDS represents, perhaps, the most empirically accurate and valuable reconstruction of the history of the party in the 1980s. The study has at least two substantial merits: it shows how the new revisionist identity of the party was underpinned by 'the underlying process of European integration along neo-liberal lines' and how it was carried out 'in parallel to the transition process to the Second Italian Republic'.[7] It also points out the importance that the 1980s had in the party's history, so dismissing the 'Iron-Link' thesis according to which the years from the collapse of the 'historic compromise' to the transformation into the PDS should be regarded as 'residual'. Nevertheless, the results of Fouskas's work are misleading in presenting the transformation of the PCI into the PDS in terms of continuity, by reducing this transition to a process through which the party's alleged 'traditional duplicity' between communism and social democracy reached an end, thanks to the definitive victory of one of its 'souls' over the other.

Although I agree with Fouskas that the transformation of the party's international and domestic policy directions—begun under Berlinguer's leadership and completed by the *Quarantenni* (the forty-year olds)—marked the history of the transition from the PCI to the PDS, I do not agree with his core thesis that this process must be understood in terms of continuity. Rather, my thesis is that, after the launching of the 'democratic alternative', the 1980s must be read in terms of discontinuity with the party's previous history. In fact I will argue that by the time of the XVI Congress in 1983, the erosion of the PCI's (at least proclaimed) hegemonic project of the transition to socialism, entailing the *fuoriuscita dal capitalismo* (exit from capitalism), had reached a point of no return, as a result of two parallel and connected processes: first, Berlinguer's gradual deradicalisation of his new strategy, and the consequent weakening of the ideological values which underpinned it; second, the simultaneous gradual penetration of values and political models closer to the liberal than to the communist tradition.

The launch of the 'democratic alternative'

Despite the steady increase in electoral support enjoyed by the PCI up to the peak of its electoral success in 1976, it had become evident by the end of the 1970s that this had little to do with electors sharing a communist vision of the future; instead the gathering momentum of secularisation and modernisation in Italian society was generating attitudes and aspirations among many of its new electors at odds with any serious socialist project.

In this respect, the '*marcia dei 40,000*' (the march of the 40,000) in 1980, when clerical workers and technicians at FIAT in Turin demanded a return to work against the strike promoted by the communist orientated trade unions, represented an important piece of evidence both for the increasing erosion of solidarity within the labour sphere, and for the diminishing feasibility of any political project anchored in the proletarian standpoint.[8] Yet, the main factor which undermined the PCI leadership's faith in the party's hegemonic project was the realisation that 'the political' could no longer be conceived of as 'directing' society. The long-term communist strategy for hegemony had been anchored in the conviction that the mass parties were able to shape the country according to the teleological dimensions of 'the political'. This had also been the conviction expressed with unmistakable force during the work of the Constituent Assembly between 1946 and 1947. The Socialist deputy Lelio Basso, working on the drafting committee for the Constitution, made an historically significant speech in which he argued that the Constituents' aim was not the construction of a liberal democracy but rather of a 'party democracy'. Within this perspective, the political vote became the expression of a world view rather than of the individual interests of single citizens, and mass parties represented 'the highest expression of democracy' insofar as they enabled millions of people to participate in the political process of shaping and organising the life of the country.[9] Further, mass parties were not the mere embodiment of a political programme, but rather the interpreters and the expressions of 'a complex and multiform reality'.[10] Berlinguer's 'historic compromise', proclaimed in 1973, was meant to seize the first opportunity in Italy's post-war history to make Lelio Basso's original proclamation a reality, and promote a cross-party guiding role in Italian society, in a progressive direction.

By the late 1970s–early 1980s, the open anti-communism of Craxi's PSI, and the introduction into the programme of the DC of the '*preambolo*' at the party XVI Congress of February 1980 where the Christian Democrats excluded any possibility of a return to collaboration with the PCI, demonstrated the definitive impracticability of this idea.[11] As a consequence, in an interview with Eugenio Scalfari, in September 1980, Berlinguer made a clear distinction between the Moro-La Malfa government of the mid 1970s (one of the experiments of the so-called Centre-Left governmental alliance between DC and PSI, with its origins in 1963) which could have opened the road to 'more advanced solutions', and the then current Cossiga government (a DC government) which had no direction and was leading the country to a state of political decay. To Berlinguer this was not simply a government with regressive policies, but expressed 'the abandonment of any political vision for leading the country with ideals and a sense of morality transcending the politics of pragmatism and immediate electoral appeal'.[12]

Accordingly, on 27 November 1980, after the disastrously ineffectual response of the government to the earthquake in Southern Italy, and in the aftermath of its 'negative and disappointing responses to the series of scandals and corrupt practices in the State apparatus', the leadership of the PCI declared that 'the moral question' was now 'the most important national issue'. This meant that the country could no longer be governed, or its problems resolved, without the restoration of 'a relationship of firm trust between citizen and state'. Therefore, since the DC had proved unable 'to give a lead in restoring a sense of morality and renewal in the state', the communists had to put themselves forwards as 'a force able to promote better government', and implement 'a programme of moral renewal and state reorganisation'. The document emphasised 'the exceptional nature of the proposal' as well as the fact that it did not express a new long-term project, but rather that its proposals would have to be realised 'within well defined time limits'.[13]

It is well known to historians of the PCI that leadership statements have to be read with great care and through the party's coded language. In the case of the proposal of the new strategy, political commentators have not paid sufficient attention to the exceptional nature of some of its key elements. The latter are, however, crucial for understanding that the 'democratic alternative' was intended as neither an ideological nor a merely tactical u-turn in the party's strategy. Of course, there was nothing 'exceptional' about the fact that the PCI was proposing itself as the country's guiding force, which, in fact, had been a constant feature of its strategy from the Salerno u-turn onwards. Nor did the proposal mean the definitive rejection of the core idea of the 'historic compromise'. At the famous press conference in Salerno on 28 November 1980, and on numerous occasions subsequently, Berlinguer made it clear that the launching of the 'democratic alternative' did not mean the abandonment of the idea of governing with, rather than against, the DC. As he warned:

> it is one thing to say, as we have done, that the DC is no longer able to guide the country. But it is another to exclude all relations with those honest elements in the DC able to take advanced positions.

Accordingly, Berlinguer emphasised the fact that the communists' 'democratic alternative' differed from the PSI's idea of the 'left alternative' insofar as the former 'visualised governing even with parties not on the left but which are nevertheless faithful to the Republican Constitution'.[14]

What in reality was 'exceptional' was the fact that the communist leadership was, at least temporarily, suspending the PCI's long-term project aimed at the hegemonisation of society for a transition to socialism, in order to concentrate all the party's energies on a short-term and more pragmatic task: campaigning for the renewal of political parties and state institutions for the more immediate need to restore governability. This was essential because within the existing state of governmental degradation to which the country had sunk, the communist project to inject a strong teleological guiding element into 'the political' was not possible. Thus, as Berlinguer said, though the party's strategy of the 'historic compromise' remained 'valid in its basic fundamentals', the necessity for the 'democratic alternative' lay 'in changes in the situation' characterising political society and 'in the pessimistic analysis' that the PCI presented of this situation:[15]

> One can understand nothing about our initiative unless one grasps the novelty of the situation. We have to face reality head on. For the first time in thirty years the risk of an institutional crisis, to the point of a collapse of the republic, has became a reality.[16]

And in fact, although the 'moral question' had been in existence for a long time, at this point, 'the recovery of trust in the institutions and in the retention of effective and democratic government' depended entirely on its solution.[17]

My argument is that the communist conception of the 'democratic alternative', although initially conceived as 'exceptional' and 'temporary' rather than a break with the previous strategy, was subsequently invested with an increasing loss of faith, on the part of the Berlinguerian leadership in the feasibility of the transition to socialism in any foreseeable future. This thesis will be confirmed by an analysis of Berlinguer's declarations between the launching of the 'democratic alternative' in 1980 to his intervention at the PCI's XVI Congress in 1983. Yet, this gradual 'loss of faith' of the communist leadership, which reached a point of no return by that congress, must not be seen as the only determinant of the erosion and fragmentation of the PCI's communist identity. Party membership was in decline, and the '*Quarantenni*', who would take over the party leadership before the end of the decade, were tottering in uncertainty. All these factors had contributed to the Berlinguerian leadership's 'loss of faith', not so much in the inherent validity and desirability of the project for a transition to socialism, as in its feasibility and likelihood.

Interpretations and re-interpretations of the 'democratic alternative'

The launching of the 'democratic alternative'—intended by the Berlinguerian leadership as the necessary premise for allowing the party to carry on with its original ideological project—had the unintended consequences of reinforcing the revisionist trends in the party. Those supporting these trends interpreted the new strategy as a substantial move towards the party's 'normalisation' (social-democratisation), which would work in tandem with a reform of the political system according to the pluralist model of alternation in government between de-ideologised parties, a model which an increasing number of party members were identifying as democracy *tout court*. This revisionist perspective was clearly represented by those people who, as Berlinguer observed, argued that the PCI should become '*un partito d'opinione*' ('a non-ideological party') whose efforts should be aimed at increasing electoral support rather than recruiting militants.[18] Accordingly, the PCI had to become a party in which all the progressive movements could find space, and reflect their objectives. Such a vision of an electoral party, reflecting the objectives of those whose support it could capture, would inevitably shift the centre of gravity of its focus away from its own vision of the society it wished to shape. This was one step away from the objective of 'capturing the middle ground' of the electorate wherever this might be, effectively adapting to the course of events and abandoning any strong ideological intent to determine them. The eventual abandonment of the PCI's communist past was clearly inscribed within such a vision of development.

This interpretation of the 'democratic alternative' is a clear reflection of the gradual rise to the top levels of party leadership and intelligentsia of a new revisionist political culture. This originally belonged to those who had been socialised in the protest movements, or who were generationally closer to the culture giving rise to these movements than to that of the party's establishment, and who had been recruited by the PCI from the 1960s onwards. By the end of the 1970s this generation formed one quarter of the party's '*functionaries*' in which, as Hellman observes, 'there were probably too many disparate interests to satisfy with any single package of proposals'.[19] With this generation, the notion of socialism no longer consisted of an all-embracing teleological project, had lost its ideological dimension, and the personal advantages and freedoms offered by a reformed capitalism seemed preferable to the uncertain prospects offered by continuing the struggle against or the 'exit' from, capitalism. The characteristics of socialism were overshadowed by those of a capitalist society which could be increasingly democratised. Authentic democracy began to be seen as a socio-political structure in which everybody was respected for his/her ideas and aspirations, with equal opportunity to participate in the political process of decision-making and access to the free market.[20] This did not mean that the younger generation of those who would become the *Quarantenni* associated with Occhetto's so-called 'Copernican Revolution'—and whose cultural break with previous communist generations is well identified by Stephen Gundle —had understood the nature of the ideologically subversive potential they were transporting into the party.[21] It was only following the doubts of the leadership itself—about the historical possibility of their strategy's success, rather than its ideological validity—after Berlinguer's death, and with the subsequent erosion of democratic centralism, that the process of ideological erosion began to have visible effect.

In open criticism of these revisionists leanings, Berlinguer's article on the '*Rinnovamento della politica e rinnovamento del PCI*' ('Renewal of politics and renewal of the PCI'), published in *Rinascita* on 4 December 1981, clearly showed his awareness of where they would all lead. He rejected them as perspectives that would reduce the party to 'a purely electoral party, an "American-type party" which would deprive political activity of all meaning'. As he argued, this kind of party—that is to say a party which tends to reflect people's needs and aspirations as they stand, rather than leading society towards a teleological project—could not be defined as a communist party. Yet, he did not deny the PCI's need for renewal, which should be carried out by a critical revision of traditional conceptions of the social struggle and of social life grounded in 'those masses, organisations and movements which represent the economic needs and demands of a trade-union type'. The traditional communist standpoint, he admitted, is in danger of excluding from the party's agenda those 'political needs and problems which are no less important and decisive for the future of the country', felt by those masses and organisations representing the socially-culturally-politically marginalised and oppressed, but outside the sphere of organised labour.[22]

These statements signalled the fact that the party secretary himself felt that the proletarian standpoint, as it was originally conceived, was increasingly less effective in a modernised and secularised Italian society. Though Berlinguer did not mean that the communist struggle should neglect the economic base and the anti-capitalist struggle, the effect of his shift of perspective was to strengthen those new revisionist tendencies towards replacing the goal of the obliteration of capitalism and transition to socialism with an agenda aimed at the democratisation of the capitalist system within social-democratic parameters. These trends gathered momentum in the party as Berlinguer's conception of the 'democratic alternative' became increasingly associated with the non-feasibility of the proletarian standpoint. As a result, the 'democratic alternative' became progressively detached from the anti-capitalist features of the previous strategy of the 'historic compromise'. As we will see, during the period between its launching in 1980 and the XVI Congress of the PCI in 1983, the proposal started to lose its anti-capitalist dimension even in the words of the party secretary himself. Inevitably, it began to coincide with the social-democratic perspective of alternation in government based on winning electoral victory, an idea which, despite the PCI's long-standing acceptance of this form of electoral politics, had never been accepted as the key element in the transition to a socialist society.

That the ideological erosion of the 'democratic alternative' was not consciously intended by Berlinguer clearly appears from the strenuous defence of the party's 'diversity', on which the secretary constantly insisted from the early 1980s until his death in 1984. However, in practice he did shift the main features of this communist 'diversity' from a clear anti-capitalist profile to the PCI's detachment from the Christian Democrat's corrupt system of power. He increasingly relegated anti-capitalist issues, and the values of socialism, to the international sphere, within which, the 'third way'—understood as something that, though different from social democracy, did not coincide with the Soviet model of communism—was constantly proclaimed as the core strategy of the party.[23] By contrast, even when he stated that the PCI had not ceased 'to pursue [anti-capitalist] objectives and to struggle for a radical transformation of society' in accordance with Marx's goal of the realisation of 'a society of "the free and the equal"' as a result of a struggle carried out by men and women 'to themselves control "the production of their conditions of life"'; even when he clearly restated the 'anomaly' which differentiated the party both from other communist parties and from social democracy; even when he rejected definitions of the party which implied that it 'resigns itself to operating within the limits of the "restrictions" established by the structures of the existing society', he defined it in accordance with an ideological conception tending towards 'a radical critique of existing society' and 'a serious consideration of "the values" which should inspire a more just society'.[24] One did not need to be a Marxist to make such statements. There was a visible, even if clearly uncomfortable, shift of perspective. One can even trace a weakening of the 'shaping' versus 'reflecting' society opposition, so fundamental to any teleological project, and to the difference between communist and social-democratic conceptions of politics.

In his statements during this final and crucial period of his leadership, Berlinguer gradually tended to reduce 'the need for the party to be active also on the ethical and social terrain', and its opposition to 'accumulation for its own sake', to the need to 'work out objectives which meet the needs for new developments manifest in society', rather than insist on a strong strategy of progressive hegemonisation in accordance with the final goal of the transition to socialism.[25]

So the parameters according to which economic development had to be shaped made no reference to the formula 'elements of socialism', which had been the core-principles of the strategy of the 1970s. They were now identified with the new needs of the existing, rather than a 'projected' future society. This change was undoubtedly temporary in Berlinguer's own mind, with the future moral and institutional configuration still needing to be resolved, but to many it seemed a clear signal and encouraged the idea that socialism was an anachronism and that the party could no longer lead the social movements according to its own 'strong' ideology. The political equivalent of the Italian postmodern philosopher Gianni Vattimo's attack on metaphysical systems had been set in train, and the PCI had begun its stumbling lurch into its own version of 'weak thought'. This interpretation is confirmed by the fact that the paradigms that Berlinguer indicated for 'a profound renewal of both the directions and structures of the system' were those along which Swedish social democracy was developing and by which 'almost half of German social-democracy, above all women and youth' and, at least to a certain extent, Mitterrand's programme, had been inspired.[26] Thus, Berlinguer was clearly making use of social-democratic reformist parameters, and this was widely interpreted as a clear signal of his adherence to the ideologically weaker social-democratic perspective.

Nor was such an interpretation of Berlinguer's intentions limited to those in the lower ranks of party membership. In his book *Per il nuovo PCI*, which, though published in 1985, was conceived soon after the XVI Congress of the party in 1983, the man who at that time was the director of the Gramsci Institute depicted Berlinguer's launching of the 'democratic alternative', not as a temporary 'suspension' of the party's ideological project, but rather as a 'sudden and drastic change of course', a dramatic u-turn of the party's strategy which 'definitively and formally' abandoned the 'historic compromise'.[27] So Berlinguer, who had doggedly defended the party's line of the 1970s even after withdrawing from the government of national solidarity, 'in a single stroke' radically changed his mind in the last months of 1980, because he 'had ceased to believe that one could set in motion a "revolutionary" process in Italy, or that it was possible to construct Socialism'.[28]

Accordingly, the 'democratic alternative' was never for Berlinguer 'a strategy for the construction of Socialism, for an anti-capitalist "revolution"', but rather, 'a programme for the political renewal of the country and for long awaited reforms'.[29] It is interesting to observe that, already in 1981, two other scholars, Marzio Barbagli and Piergiorgio Corbetta, in their analysis of the launching of the 'democratic alternative' also saw it as 'a real u-turn', through which the party leadership abandoned the 'historic compromise' as a result of that 'profound process of change and renewal within both the base and the activists in the party', which the authors describe 'as a gust of fresh air ...blowing through the closed doors of the party branches' through 'new forces, with different political pasts from those of the preceding generations' that 'have brought into doubt and in part changed the old mentalities and life-styles'.[30]

Within this perspective, the fact that—though with an ambiguity of language uncharacteristic of his past leadership—Berlinguer was still defending the idea that his party could be defined as 'a real socialist party' in the sense that the PCI was 'serious about constructing socialism', is explained by arguing that he never openly declared the ideological change that the new strategy implied for two reasons: first because of the traditional 'continuism' which had characterised the entire party's history; second, for fear of the repercussions it could have within the PCI's leadership.[31] For this reason, he was never able to give 'strategic breadth to the alternative' and to build 'around it a general vision, a coherent project, a new source of inspiration'.[32]

Although it is difficult to endorse the view of a total and sudden conversion to social democracy on the part of Berlinguer, the present article does argue that Berlinguer's ambiguities must be seen in one sense as the signal of a gradual loss of faith in the feasibility of a political project based on communist values at least in the foreseeable future. But there was also a growing willingness to concede that the process of capitalist colonisation had gone so far that social-democratic paradigms constituted the only model through which the values of solidarity could, at least for the present, be opposed not only to those tendencies 'towards narrowness, to returning to the past and to old customs and hierarchies', but also to those 'mythicisations of "the individual" and of "the private"', that, as Berlinguer regretted, were shared by parts of the Italian left, and contained 'more than a little of that offensive which characterises the relaunching of neoliberal economic policies'.[33] It is clear from the tone of reluctance in his speeches as much as from their ambiguity, and his timid reminders of his party's real socialist mission, that to Berlinguer any move into social democracy, far from being the objective towards which the PCI had been evolving, was at worst a tragic abandonment, and at best a temporary suspension, of its goals, and in either event a capitulation to the sheer force and strength of the enemy.

In such circumstances Berlinguer himself began to reinterpret the 'democratic alternative'. His formulation—which, as I have emphasised, had not originally entailed a break with the 'historic compromise'—not only progressively abandoned the anti-capitalism which had characterised the latter, but was also gradually reduced to a governmental formula whose task was to democratise the socio-political structure rather than obliterate the capitalist nature of its economic base. Thus, whereas Berlinguer never abandoned his Communist ideals, in 1982, when speaking of the PCI's domestic policy, he clearly started to differentiate the 'historic compromise' from 'the political agenda which we established from November 1980', which consisted of 'the democratic alternative to the system of power and government rooted in the DC'.[34] So, in spite of the fact that in 1983 it was still said that 'the ideas inspiring the historic compromise remain valid', understood as 'the search for a meeting of minds and efforts in common with catholic organisations', the difference between this and the new definition of the 'democratic alternative' was clear.[35]

Berlinguer's change of mind about collaboration with the DC is easier to understand if we bear in mind some critical events which would have caused him to reconsider. When he announced the 'democratic alternative' in November 1980, the scandal over the P2 Masonic lodge and its membership had not yet erupted, the secret negotiations with the Red Brigades, leading to the ransom of Ciro Cirillo (the Christian Democrat politician kidnapped on April 1981) had not yet been reported, and Dalla Chiesa (the Carabineri General who is widely believed to have been deliberately sent to Palermo to combat the Mafia without sufficient protection) had not yet been assassinated. The DC was implicated in these, and other, developments which by the time of the PCI Congress in March 1983 would have cast the prospect of collaborating with a party presiding over a crumbling system of public order in a totally different light. The restoring of public confidence in government had become, to Berlinguer, an unmistakable priority.

The main indicators of a new formulation of the 'democratic alternative', in which the transition to socialism had been set aside for more immediate objectives, can be identified in two different factors: first, the common ground that Berlinguer indicated for collaboration with Catholic movements consisted less of those values of solidarity that the communist and catholic ideologies could share, than of the non-ideological and more pragmatic 'desire to affirm greater honesty and moral probity in public and private life, a need to reform the state and party organisations'.[36] Second, but most important, the Secretary declared that, whereas the 'historic compromise' entailed 'collaboration with the DC also at government level, the democratic alternative excludes this'.[37] Though Berlinguer never admitted a clear break with the previous theorisation against governing with 50 per cent + 1 of the votes, he declared that the party no longer rejected this option.[38]

The PCI's original rejection of the 50 per cent + 1 electoral formula as a sufficient basis for governing the country was based on the fact that the party's objective was the 'exit from capitalism', not its reform. A government of the left supported by 50 per cent + 1 of the votes would be forced to work within the terms of the accepted social order, and could not subvert it. In the first place, when an electoral victory of the PCI was being thought of as a possibility in 1976, it was clear that much of the new support for the party was not based on its anti-capitalism. Alone in power, it would have had the major capitalist forces against it, with their economic and media power to thwart any major subversive initiatives. The only possible route towards fundamental structural anti-capitalist transformations was with, and not against, political forces leading the masses. At the time, Berlinguer judged that the DC led sufficient numbers, and had still retained enough of its anti-fascist and Catholic culture of solidarity, to make such co-operation possible. Thus, Berlinguer's new-found willingness to accept an electoral formula as sufficient for government in the early 1980s, in which a government with the DC was no longer feasible, necessarily implied at the very least a temporary suspension of the party's ultimate goal of the 'exit from capitalism'. In fact, the corruption and inefficiency which now clearly characterised the political society of that period denied the necessary premises for this objective, namely a solid link between political and civil societies. Therefore, the goal of introducing 'elements of socialism' into the socio-political structure had to be suspended in order to concentrate all the energies of the party on arresting the dramatic decline of 'the political'.

Accordingly, ten years after the Chilean coup, which had provided the international background to the 'historic compromise', though he was still arguing that, in the 1980s,

> any formation on the left, which deludes itself that it can manage, within a Western democratic capitalist government, to steer a stable and successful course of government, and manage 'orderly' economic and financial policies, even though static and within the system as it stands, must be prepared, sooner or later to have its actions rejected by the working, popular masses whose trust a party of the left must retain.[39]

Berlinguer hardly mentioned the need to hegemonise the working class, or the ultimate goal of the 'exit from capitalism'. Accordingly, even the way in which the 'objective contadiction' of the situation described above could be resolved was very vague and confused, and the concept of renewal appeared untheorised:

> it can be done if one wishes to resolve it by innovation (including oneself), or, alternatively, by some hard thinking, that is by theoretical elaboration; by some creative political initiatives breaking through established patterns and sacred cows in order to free oneself from prejudice, opportunism and all forms of maximalist rigidity.[40]

Berlinguer's call to 'reinsert into politics "long-term visions", projects… supported by a rigorous analysis of social reality' in order to avoid 'empty, rhetorical pronouncements' no longer seemed to be inspired by those anti-capitalist goals which had characterised the Italian Road to Socialism until the late 1970s.[41] It was now hardly distinguishable from a social-democratic perspective according to which everybody should benefit from economic, social and cultural advancements, independent of the obliteration of the capitalist nature of the economic base. In fact, in 1983, Berlinguer's definition of socialism was:

> the conscious and democratic, therefore non-authoritarian and repressive, management of economic and social processes aimed at balanced development, social justice, and at the cultural development of the whole of humanity.[42]

Thus, by 1983, the values and ultimate goals of the transition to socialism had started to become, even to Berlinguer, personal ideals rather than the basis of a feasible political project. The conception of the party as the agency for shaping, rather than merely reflecting, people's aspirations, was becoming weaker and weaker, and the Italian Road to Socialism was becoming less and less distinguishable from a project focused on the democratisation of capitalism.

The XVI Congress of the PCI

It could be argued that the thesis that I have presented is contradicted by Berlinguer's report to the XVI Congress of the party in 1983, and by the political document approved on that occasion. From the words of both the secretary and the congress policy document the PCI leadership still seemed firmly convinced of the validity of the transition to socialism. Berlinguer clearly distinguished between a struggle inspired by the revolutionary goals of socialism and one aimed at 'other objectives, even important and noble, but less advanced, more empirical, non revolutionary'.[43] He concluded that it was still worth struggling for this objective, despite a campaign meant to 'eradicate from the consciousness of the masses and from serious intellectual reflections and analysis the idea that capitalism can and must be overcome and replaced by a society inspired by socialist aims'.[44] The political document came to an even firmer conclusion: 'the need for socialism …presents itself as a need of history'.[45] Furthermore, it argued that the 'democratic alternative'—by bringing forward both a new leading class 'endowed with a sense of nation and state', and a reforming force able to overcome the crisis and to transform the country 'in a fully democratic, modern, efficient, juster and freer manner'— represented the strategy by which it was possible to 'put into motion a process of transformation in a socialist direction'.[46]

Yet, despite such strong statements, if we analyse these documents, we cannot fail to detect a profound lowering of anti-capitalist morale and tone. Despite still claiming the transition to socialism as the party's ultimate goal, Berlinguer depicted the acquisition by the working class and the popular forces of a consciousness shaped by the values of solidarity as a hypothesis which was far from being realised. As he clearly pointed out, the Western working class, along with the other emancipatory movements, was less and less concerned with those 'gigantic processes of world and national economic restructuring', which were vital for the socialist cause, and more and more focused on the defence of those mostly material advantages which had been achieved during the previous decade:

> until the working class, the popular masses and all the more far-sighted forces working for democracy and peace operating in the Northen hemisphere gain a full awareness of the importance in general and concrete terms of the North–South problem, the construction of a new, united international economic order will struggle to advance. Furthermore, the same problems in the economic and social lives of countries in the North will end up in stagnation. The Western workers' movement itself, if it thinks simply in terms of defending the gains of the last decades, will not be able to avoid their erosion and the undermining of its own trade-union and political positions.[47]

Gramsci's 'pessimism of the intellect' is certainly evident in this analysis, but the 'optimism of the will', which to Gramsci was always the sign of a genuine desire for revolutionary transformation, has been totally sapped. The working-class conquests of the past, traditionally presented in communist speeches in an optimistic light, and as stimuli for forward movement in a socialist direction, have become instead seductive traps for the unwary, and the working class and its allies are presented in the gloomy light of the self-satisfied whose sense of collective identity has almost been extinguished.

The same concern underlay the political document stating that 'a greater degree of development' could be realised only if 'the sources of the splits and divisions among the workers' could be overcome.[48] The congress called for the unity of the working class with the new strata emerging from the technologisation of the labour sphere, and suggested that for this purpose the party should contribute 'to the indispensable formation of the new political consciousness [of the workers]'.[49] Yet, it was conceded that, due to social and economic transformations, it was no longer possible to construct the unity of labour on the basis of what all the different categories of workers had in common but, by contrast, it was necessary to 'focus on the specific roles and functions of these categories in order to promote greater development in the civic and productive spheres'.[50] This apparent injection of what commentators have seen as a 'realistic' acceptance of the differences in the composition of the working class, in effect contained a more profound, and demoralising realisation that it was difficult, if at all possible, to mobilise on the simple basis of class solidarity. Moreover, the participation of the various 'progressive' strata in the construction of the 'democratic alternative' had to be not only 'wide', but also 'autonomous'.[51] Accordingly, when speaking about the women's movement—though it was argued that the 'the objectives of women's liberation' must be connected to 'struggles in the field of production'—it was concluded that all the 'new movements', inspired by goals like:

> the protection of minorities, the participation of those masses until recently excluded from areas of cultural life, support for the addicted and other marginalised groups, struggles for a better quality of life, the protection and improvement of the natural and cultural environment, support for the ecological movement, respect for choices in life-style, the rejection of all forms of discrimination, solidarity with the disabled.[52]

Those goals should contribute to renew not only politics and society, but also the political parties, which in turn must understand 'the autonomous demands of these movements and give them real political expression in society'.[53]

Conclusion

It is quite evident that, though the congress did not admit that the socio-economic transformations were increasingly denying the feasibility of the anti-capitalist proletarian standpoint, the communist leadership was gradually losing faith in it, and was trying to accommodate the aspirations of a fragmented and de-ideologised society. Accordingly, Berlinguer's and the political document's attempts to maintain the proletarian standpoint and the struggle against economic exploitation were undermined by key factors: the idea of 'autonomy' seemed to have replaced that of 'hegemony' under the progressive leadership of the working class; it seemed that the unity of progressive forces, rather than converge on the ideological values and ultimate goals of the ideal future socialist society, had to focus on objectives such as relaunching forms of economic development 'free from restrictive government policies, from the squandering of public finances and in favour of technological modernisation'.[54] Whereas the 'austerity policy' of the mid-1970s had posited such objectives within a more global framework of economic transformation, these goals now seemed to be accepted as free-floating instruments for the achievement of economic efficiency in its own right. The anti-capitalist ideological goals of a transformation aimed at introducing 'elements of socialism' was now increasingly replaced by pragmatic objectives aimed at 'governability' and economic efficiency.

Thus, in saying that by the XVI Congress the process of erosion of the Communist identity had reached a point of no return, I do not mean that there was a clear-cut and conscious break with all that the party had stood for, but rather that, by 1983, the political project of the communist leadership was no longer characterised by a strong faith in the feasibility of the original hegemonic project of a transition to socialism. The fragmentation of the PCI's communist identity must be understood as the result of two parallel and interrelated processes: the speedy decline of communist faith in the original teleological project, reflected in the increasing pragmatism of Berlinguer's conception of the 'democratic alternative'; and the gradual infusion into the party's leadership and/or intelligentsia of a new political culture and agenda, which, at least until the late 1970s, had been extraneous and even irreconcilable with the ideological values and ultimate goals inspiring the PCI's anti-capitalist project. This penetration would have been much more difficult without the first factor, and was greatly reinforced by the space which the launching and the development of the 'democratic alternative' opened up for a revisionist interpretation of the party's new line.

Notes

1. See for example: Luciano Cafagna, *C'era una volta...Riflessioni sul comunismo italiano* (Venice, 1991); Marcello Flores and Nicola Gallerano, *Sul PCI. Un'interpretazione storica* (Bologna, 1992); Giorgio Galli, *Storia del PCI. Il Partito comunista italiano: Livorno 1921, Rimini 1991* (Milan, 1993); Piero Ignazi, *Dal PCI al PDS* (Bologna, 1992); Luciano Pellicani, *Gramsci, Togliatti e il PCI. Dal moderno Principe al post-comunismo* (Rome, 1990).
2. This view can be found in: Joan Barth Urban, 'Gorbachev's state visit to Italy and the Vatican', in F. Sabetti and R. Catanzaro (eds) *Italian Politics: A Review*, 5 (London and Wolfeboro, NH, 1991), pp.126–37; Urban, 'The PCI's 17th Congress: a Triumph of the "New Internationalism"', in R.Y. Nanetti, R. Leonardi and P. Corbetta (eds) *Italian Politics: A Review*, 2 (London and Wolfeboro, NH, 1988), pp.41–52; Martin Bull, 'Whatever Happened to Italian Communism? Explaining the dissolution of the largest communist party in the West', *West European Politics*, 14 (1991), pp.96–120; Vassilis Fouskas, *Italy, Europe, the Left. The transformation of Italian communism and the European imperative* (Aldershot, Brookfield, Singapore and Sydney, 1998); Stephen Hellman, *Italian Communism in Transition* (New York and Oxford, 1988); Stephen Hellman, 'The Italian Communist party between Berlinguer and the Seventeenth Congress', in R. Leonardi, and Y. Nanetti (eds) *Italian Politics: A Review*, 1 (London and Wolfeboro NH, 1986), pp.47–68; Donald Sassoon, 'The 1987 Elections and the PCI', in R. Leonardi and P. Corbetta (eds) *Italian Politics: A Review*, 3 (London and New York, 1989), pp.129–45.
3. From the standpoint of discontinuity, within the 'Evolutionary' perspective, see Bull, 'Whatever Happened to Italian Communism?'; within the 'Iron-Link' perspective see Ignazi, *Dal PCI al PDS*.
4. Grant Amyot, 'The PCI and Occhetto's New Course: the Italian road to reform', in R.Y. Nanetti and R. Catanzaro (eds) *Italian Politics: A Review*, 4 (London and New York, 1990), pp.146–61.
5. Flores, Gallerano, *Sul PCI*, p.258.
6. Bull, 'Whatever Happened to Italian Communism?', p.109.
7. Fouskas, *Italy, Europe, the Left*, p.xv.
8. For more detail see Gino Bedani, *Politics and Ideology in the Italian Workers' Movement* (Oxford, 1995), pp.252–6.
9. *La Costituzione della Repubblica nei lavori preparatori della Assemblea Costituente*, 1 (Rome: Camera dei Deputati, Segretariato Generale, 1970), p.207. All translations of Italian texts into English are by the author, unless otherwise stated.
10. *La Costituzione della Repubblica*, p.208. It should be pointed out that the Catholics on the drafting committee were in full agreement with this view. See Gino Bedani, 'Pluralism, Integralism and the Framing of the Republican Constitution in Italy: the Role of the Catholic Left', in *Sguardi sull'Italia. Miscellania dedicata a Francesco Villari*, G. Bedani, et al. (eds) (Leeds: Society for Italian Studies, 1997), pp.158–70.

11. On the rise of Craxi in 1976 and on his anti-historic compromise positions see Piero Craveri, *La Repubblica dal 1958 al 1992* (Turin, 1995), pp.662–72 and 674–8; On the so called 'DC del preambolo', see Craveri, *La Repubblica*, pp.818–19; Agostino Giovagnoli, *Il partito Italiano. La Democrazia Cristiana dal 1942 al 1999* (Bari and Rome, 1996), pp.201–6.
12. Enrico Berlinguer, '"Socialismo realizzato" e rivoluzione in occidente', Interview with E. Scalari, *La Repubblica*, 26 September 1980, p.202. Reprinted in A. Tatò (ed.), *Conversazioni con Berlinguer* (Rome, 1984), pp.186–204.
13. PCI, Document approved by the Direzione of the PCI on the 27 November 1980, in *Conversazioni con Berlinguer*, pp.212–13.
14. Berlinguer, 'Terremoto ed emergenza politica', transcription of the conference in Salerno on the 28 November 1980, in *Conversazioni con Berlinguer*, pp.211–14. See also Berlinguer, 'L'alternativa democratica', interview with A. Reichlin. *L'Unità*, 7 December 1980, reprinted in *Conversazioni con Berlinguer*, pp.215–23.
15. Berlinguer, 'L'alternativa democratica', p.216.
16. Berlinguer, 'L'alternativa democratica', p.218.
17. Berlinguer, 'L'alternativa democratica', p.218.
18. Berlinguer, 'Rinnovamento della politica e rinnovamento del PCI', *Rinascita*, 4 December 1981, pp.11–13.
19. Piero Ignazi, *Il potere dei partiti. La politica in Italia dagli anni Sessanta a oggi* (Bari and Rome, 2002), p.52; Chiara Sebastiani, 'I funzionari', in A. Accornero, R. Mannheimer, C. Sebastiani (eds) *L'identità comunista. I militanti, la struttura e la cultura del PCI* (Rome, 1983), pp.79–177, 144–71; Hellman, *Italian Communism in Transition*, p.32. It should be noted that both the 'Iron-Link' and the 'Evolutionary' perspective acknowledge the role that the new generation of militants, cadres and leaders exerted on the process of the party's transformation. For the 'Iron Link' perspective, see for example Ignazi, *Il potere dei partiti. La politica in Italia dagli anni Sessanta a oggi* (Bari and Rome, 2002), pp.82–3. For the 'evolutionary' perspective see Stephen Hellman, 'Italian Communism in the First Republic', in S. Gundle and S. Parker (eds), *The New Italian Republic. From the fall of the Berlin wall to Berlusconi* (London, 1996), pp.72–84.
20. This was not, of course, an overnight conversion of all PCI members, many of whom resisted this trend. It does, however, describe the gathering momentum of the rapidly shifting centre of gravity of the party.
21. See Gundle, *Between Hollywood and Moscow* (Durham and London, 2000), pp.164–210.
22. Berlinguer, 'Rinnovamento della politica e rinnovamento del PCI', p.12.
23. See for example Berlinguer, 'Discorso di Enrico Berlinguer ai lavoratori Fiat. Risposta operaia alla crisi', *L'Unità*, 16 February 1981, pp.1–2. On that occasion Berlinguer still called for 'a profound transformation within the economy, society, political parties and also in ideas' against the attempt, by the 'dominant capitalist groups and privileged classes', to reduce 'the social importance' and 'the gains' of the working class 'restricting their rights and freedoms…seeking

to corrupt the ideals and politics of the working class', by attempting 'to deprive it of its self awareness, and of its consciousness as a class'. The 'peculiarity' that the party opposed to this agenda was clearly focused on the party's 'new conception of internationalism'; the PCI 'proposes a "third way" seen as an advance on the stages and roads pursued by the workers' movements and its parties up to now, both in the West and in the East, and also aimed at a convergence of popular, and working-class forces in Western Europe' (p.2).

24. Berlinguer, 'La nostra diversità', Interview with L. Barca, in *Critica marxista*, 2 (1981). *Reprinted in Conversazioni con Berlinguer*, pp.224–38.
25. Berlinguer, 'La nostra diversità', p.238.
26. Berlinguer, 'Che cos'è la questione morale', interview with E. Scalari, La Repubblica, 28 July 1981, reprinted in *Conversazioni con Berlinguer*, pp.250–69.
27. Aldo Schiavone, *Per il nuovo PCI* (Bari and Rome, 1985), p.102.
28. Schiavone, *Per il nuovo PCI*, p.108.
29. Schiavone, *Per il nuovo PCI*, p.112.
30. Marzio Barbagli and Piergiorgio Corbetta, 'La svolta del PCI', *Il Mulino*, 273 (1981), pp.95–130.
31. Berlinguer, 'Che cos'è la questione morale', p.256; Schiavone, *Per il nuovo PCI*, p.110.
32. Schiavone, *Per il nuovo PCI*, p.112.
33. Berlinguer, 'La nostra diversità', pp.236, 238.
34. See also Berlinguer, 'Un ritratto televisivo', interview with G. Minoli, *Mixer*, Rai Due, 27 April 1983, reprinted in *Conversazioni con Berlinguer*, pp.316–29; Berlinguer, 'Otto risposte a Moravia', interview with A. Moravia, in *Nuovi argomenti*, 2 (1982), reprinted in *Conversazioni con Berlinguer*, pp.286–96.
35. Berlinguer, 'Un ritratto televisivo', p.317.
36. Berlinguer, 'Comunisti e cattolici nella crisi attuale', Adista (Agenzia di informazione stampa), 2525–7, 16–18 December 1982, reprinted in *Conversazioni con Berlinguer*, pp.304–15.
37. Berlinguer, 'Un ritratto televisivo', p.317.
38. See Berlinguer, 'Un ritratto televisivo', p.318. The difference between the 'historic compromise' and the 'democratic alternative' and the characterisation of the latter as a governmental perspective rather than as a teleological project is stated even more clearly in Enrico Berlinguer, 'A dieci anni dal golpe in Cile', *La Repubblica*, 11 September 1983, reprinted in *Conversazioni con Berlinguer*, pp.344–8. Here Berlinguer insisted on 'the need for a democratic alternative—which in the present conditions in Italy also means putting the DC into opposition—insofar as this need has become urgent and immediate because of the degeneration of the system of government and of a style of political management which are the fruit of government coalitions with the DC at their centre' (p.345).
39. Enrico Berlinguer, 'A dieci anni dal golpe in Cile', p.347.
40. Berlinguer, 'A dieci anni dal golpe in Cile', p.347.
41. Enrico Berlinguer, 'Verso il Duemila', interview with F. Adornato, *L'Unità*, 18

December 1983, reprinted in *Conversazioni con Berlinguer*, pp.349–60.
42. Berlinguer, 'Verso il Duemila', p.358.
43. Enrico Berlinguer, 'Relazione al XVI Congresso del PCI', in Economia, stato, pace: l'iniziativa e le proposte del PCI. Rapporto, conclusioni e documento politico del XVI Congresso (Rome, 1983), pp.3–57.
44. Berlinguer, 'Relazione al XVI Congresso del PCI', pp.12–13.
45. PCI, 'Documento politico approvato dal XVI Congresso del PCI', in *Economia, stato, pace*, pp.77–172.
46. PCI, 'Documento politico approvato dal XVI Congresso del PCI', pp.81–2.
47. Berlinguer, 'Relazione al XVI Congresso del PCI', p.16.
48. PCI, 'Documento politico approvato dal XVI Congresso del PCI', pp.81–2.
49. PCI, 'Documento politico approvato dal XVI Congresso del PCI', pp.86–7.
50. PCI, 'Documento politico approvato dal XVI Congresso del PCI', p.87.
51. PCI, 'Documento politico approvato dal XVI Congresso del PCI', p.88.
52. PCI, 'Documento politico approvato dal XVI Congresso del PCI', p.90.
53. PCI, 'Documento politico approvato dal XVI Congresso del PCI', p.90.
54. PCI, 'Documento politico approvato dal XVI Congresso del PCI', p.88.

Books to Remember

A long day's journey into the night
Ralph Miliband, *Parliamentary Socialism: A study in the politics of labour*, Allen & Unwin, 1961.

Nostalgia has been an understandable temptation for the Labour Party left in a party which at all times—except perhaps briefly after 1945—has seemed to be reneging on its basic values and betraying the heritage of its past. Things were always better in the old days. Ralph Miliband's volume questioned this attitude, for it argued, the Labour Party *never* lived up to its ostensible promise, and indeed could not betray a conviction which it never had in the first place.

The problem is encapsulated in the title, *Parliamentary Socialism*—with the stress on *Parliamentary*. By committing itself to realising its vision through parliamentary institutions the Labour Party surrendered its position in advance; for this strategy required it above all to seek 'respectability' and that meant that whatever its intentions might be it had (and has) to work on terms set by the class enemy.

Miliband had first propounded the theme of the volume a year earlier with an article in the initial number of *New Left Review* under the title 'The Sickness of Labourism', possibly the first use of that term. When the book appeared in 1961 it caused a sensation as well as much indignation and embarrassment among Labour Party commentators who were outraged by Miliband's premises—and not all of the critics were on the right wing of the Labour Party. Richard Crossman, for example, reviewed it virulently in the *New Statesman*.

Miliband's key distinction was not one which commended itself to his critics, for it reversed the customary terms of debate. He identified on the one hand realists, whether on the right or left, who appreciated that politics is essentially civil war by other means (to adapt Clausewitz's famous definition) and, on the other, self-deceivers who imagine that socio-economic structures are fundamentally benign and needing only a degree (possibly even a significant degree) of adjustment.

For the privileged classes of course these structures *are* benign (though perhaps requiring a little fine tuning). For those at the sharp end of the class structure, supposedly the labour movement's core constituency, they most certainly are not. Though a reformist labour movement may succeed in improving matters from time to time—whether or not it achieves government office—the poor, and a fairly substantial number of poor at that, will always be with us.

Historical survey

Parliamentary Socialism is a history of the Labour Party written within this intellectual framework and examines how at every turn during its growth and development into a significant political power and contender for office it failed to rise to its responsibilities and measure up to the historical challenge. His opening sentence sets the tone,

> Of all political parties claiming socialism to be their aim, the Labour Party has always been one of the most dogmatic—not about socialism but about the parliamentary system.

Certainly few Labour MPs have escaped being corrupted in their political and cultural attitudes by the parliamentary embrace, but the Labour Party sprang from the trade unions and it was they who made the decision to prioritise the parliamentary road. J.H. Thomas, that sinister star of the modern labour movement's early career, whose misdeeds are detailed at length by Miliband (though even Thomas might have hesitated to drag a terminally ill woman from her deathbed and deport her out of reach of medical facilities, or to threaten the unemployed and disabled with eviction from their homes) was a trade-union leader before he was an MP.

From time to time the unions have been a odds with the parliamentary leadership but in the end have always yielded to its guidance and most of the time have been committed to the party's right wing, which in turn has been committed to Establishment values.

As early as 1908 a leading Labour MP was proposing legal restrictions on union activity, and in the very first (minority) Labour governments of the 1920s there was an eerie foreshadowing of present-day government policies with military action in Iraq (since 1919 a British 'mandate') and scandals with cash-for-honours allegations directed at the Prime Minister Ramsay MacDonald. The sorry tale continues through the 1920s and 1930s, the General Strike, the collapse of the second Labour government, MacDonald's defection to the Tories, the failure to use the movement's potential strength against fascism at home and abroad.

The Second World War changed everything and certainly resulted in a powerful flux of leftward sentiment among the public at large. At the same time, by bringing the party leaders into close working contact with Conservative colleagues in the wartime Coalition government it disposed them to a better 'understanding' of the latter's point of view.

Essentials of Labourism

Miliband describes the 1945–50 government as 'the climax of Labourism' and acknowledges the very significant social amelioration which it introduced under very difficult circumstances. At the same time he dissects the practices through which it strove to avoid giving too much offence to the opposition in Parliament and outside it, swallowed much of its opponents' notion of the national interest in domestic affairs and virtually all of it in foreign ones, and made no effort at all to dismantle the inherited structure of wealth and privilege. Above all he is concerned to stress that Attlee's administration behaved in this manner not because its ministers calculated how much would be feasible in terms of public acceptance but because they saw matters through conservative-tinted spectacles.

The Conservatives, returning to office in 1951, had no difficulty in taking on board all the social measures of 1945–50 and, in improved economic conditions, even bettered some of them. They accepted the nationalisations as well (the ones they reversed were in 1950–51), thus leaving the Labour Party at sixes and sevens, consuming itself in the Bevanite struggle, in a state of 'paralysis of ideology' as Miliband terms it, so that its leaders soon put themselves in a 'defensive, even plaintive posture'.

Miliband's indictment is comprehensive and damning—and has an evident resonance for our own times. However it could be argued that his focus on parliamentary socialism gives his analysis a somewhat idealist character. The seductions of Lords and Commons, the great offices of state and the neo-feudal milieu associated with all of that can account for a great deal —but not for the culture which continued to endorse the kind of politics that the labour movement pursued throughout the twentieth century. Occasionally Labour's public constituency was ahead of it politically, but not very often. When eventually a Labour Party nearer to Miliband's vision did emerge it proved extremely unpopular and the episode nearly destroyed it.

However were he alive today Miliband might well argue that his closing paragraph accurately predicted the kind of pressures such a remodelled party would come under (though unhappily he was wrong about the compensating advantages) and that the Labour Party was destroyed anyway, though in a somewhat different fashion from what looked likely in 1983. In 1997 the electorate voted overwhelmingly to dispose of Thatcherism, and what they actually got was Thatcherism intensified. In the early 1990s I predicted that Labour would become indistinguishable from the Liberal Democrats: it never occurred to me that it would become indistinguishable from the Tories.

Willie Thompson

Reviews

All Our Yesterdays

David Kynaston, *Austerity Britain: A World to Build* (Bloomsbury, London, 2008), ISBN 978–074757985–7, 704pp., £25.00 (hb).

David Kynaston's photographs are compelling. The Tory candidate in the 1945 election speaks to a small crowd on a bomb site in Bethnal Green. His cause was hopeless. Not so Aneurin Bevan's who stands in dark suit surveying cooling towers and smoking chimneys. Sheffield trams in the rain, Liverpool museum steps in slushy snow, the Gorbals in shades of grey. In Durham City on Miners' Gala day 1949 the crowd share devotion, celebration and sheer enjoyment. The Croxhall Lodge banner displays the Conishead Priory Convalescent Home for Miners. A Woolworth's shop window insists 'Your HOLIDAY NEEDS ARE HERE. Get them NOW'. On another bombsite a queue snakes towards Waterloo station suitcases packed for holidays in the south and south west. The sun does not shine nor does it on Margate beach where pilgrims to the sea huddle for shelter. In Blackpool at least the sky is light. A middle-aged man collar tie and three-piece suit stands primly in shallow water, shoes and socks in hand.

Austerity Britain is a composition of many voices. To listen is to relive my earliest memories. The colours of ration books, buses with slatted wooden seats, queues at the butcher, queues at the housing office, day trips by coach to the seaside, not all in the rain. 'Listen with Mother' which somehow in that 1950 summer became interwoven with English cricketers' travails at the hands of the West Indies 'those two little pals of mine-Ramadhin and Valentine'. My first political memory also came through the radio. A Friday afternoon in February 1950 my grandmother and my mother neither deeply political, listening to the election drama as Labour's overnight lead was whittled away. I remember the refrain, 'the Liberal candidate lost his deposit'.

Its meaning was obscure but there was good reason for the memory. It was the fate of 319 Liberals. More pervasively I sensed excitement. Something that I did not understand really mattered.

Somehow that memory stuck. Years later I discovered that in that February election when hours at work were longer, cars were far fewer, and polling stations could be distant, almost 84 per cent of the electorate voted. This was the highest ever turnout in Britain under a mass electoral franchise. Yet Kynaston suggests that 'it was not an election that ever really caught fire' (p. 380). This apparent paradox offers a starting point for discussion of a rich and nuanced tapestry which incorporates challenging and controversial assessments.

Facile and generalising claims about radicalisation and the homogeneity of class experiences are subverted. Attempts are made to connect political debates and choices with quotidian concerns about food shortages and the lack of decent housing, the idioms of popular radio programmes and the fortunes and misfortunes of football and cricket teams. Kynaston ends with Newcastle's 1951 Wembley victory over Blackpool the day that 'Waur Jackie' triumphed over Stanley Mathews but he also weaves in the disasters of Accrington Stanley. A Labour sympathising housewife in middle-class Chingford reflected ruefully on the way that domestic concerns shaped her election drama of February 1950.

> Had a dreadful day with babes and their colds. Kept grizzling. I tried putting Pamela to sleep but had to bring her down again when she was so weepy. To make matters worse I was straining hard to get Election Results. Made a game of it by booing Conservatives and cheering Labour, but it wore very thin before nightfall (p.391).

Kynaston offers contrasting middle-class voices. When J. G. Ballard returned to England in the spring of 1946 from internment in a Japanese camp for civilians he was bombarded by the vehemence of his family.

> All these middle-class people, my parents, friends and relations and the like, were seething with a sort of repressed rage at the world around them. And what they were raging against was the post-war Labour government. It was impossible to have any kind of dialogue about the rights and wrongs of the National Health Service, which was about to come in, they talked as if this Labour government was an occupying power, that the Bolsheviks had arrived and were to strip them of everything they owned (p.172).

As Kynaston comments 'a strong almost tribal backlash was well under way within a year of Labour taking power' (p. 172). Harold Laski makes only a marginal appearance in the text as a controversial presence in the 1945 election. But in November 1946 as the backlash gathered pace he brought an unsuccessful libel action against a local newspaper the *Newark Advertiser*. The affair encapsulated the resentments of the Conservative middle class. Laski's case was that the newspaper had reported that at a meeting in June 1945 he had acknowledged that in the last resort a Labour Government might employ violent methods to secure its objectives. The report had been provided for the editor by James Wentworth Day a high Tory of exotic and reactionary views and advisor to the local Conservative candidate. Wentworth Day had a penchant for exaggeration and in the eyes of some Conservatives misrepresentation. The defence was represented by Sir Patrick Hastings. He had been Labour's Attorney General in the 1924 Government and a leading figure in the Campbell case that had brought about that government's defeat in the Commons. This controversy and the subsequent election campaign with its anti-Bolshevism symbolised by the Zinoviev letter had its echoes in the Laski case. Hastings's Labour moment had been brief and was a distant memory. He effectively turned plaintiff into defendant. Laski was represented as the personification of an alien 'socialism'. Hastings's cross examination stroked the prejudices of a special jury recruited from a restricted and relatively affluent stratum. They had no hesitation in deciding against Laski. The *Newark Advertiser*'s editor received many congratulatory letters. One hailing this first blow against the socialist government came from the recently retired Mayor of Grantham Alderman Alfred Roberts.[1]

Kynaston queries what all the angst and vitriol was about. Through the 1940s there had been some economic redistribution. Compared with 1938 post-tax salaries in 1949 had fallen by 16 per cent whereas wages had increased by 21 per cent (p.173). This redistribution still left a decisive inequality. In 1949 a professional man's salary was equal to the combined incomes of a skilled, a semi-skilled and an unskilled workman (p.409). Beyond the anatomy of incomes the universalism of the post-war welfare settlement benefited the middle class, particularly through free secondary education and a free health service, the more so since much of the finance came from transfers of income within the working class.

Late in 1949 a correspondent wrote to *Picture Post*. Her address in impeccably suburban Heald Green indicated her social, if not her geographical, distance from the often appallingly housed Mancunian working class. Social distance co-habited with certainty. 'The Socialist Government seems to be unable to make the workers realise the seriousness of the present situation' (p.431). Her remedy was draconian—a five-and-a-half, or even six-day week at the same weekly wage, in other words a substantial wage cut. Stereotypes about working-class idleness, indifference and bloody mindedness were deeply rooted and had fuelled the Conservative Party's dominance of the interwar years. The backbone of the nation, the decent and deserving were set against the allegedly aggressive unionised section of the working class or alternatively against claimants for unemployment benefit who could be stigmatised as work shy and fraudulent.

Such prejudices were comforting. Their self-serving moralism had facilitated enjoyment of the material benefits that had resulted from the deflationary economics of the 1920s and 1930s. At least in the short term stable money incomes, falling prices, limited unemployment and low personal taxation had served the interests of the professions and suburbia. Thus Orwell surveyed sleek southern England from the boat train on his return from Spain in mid 1937. 'The industrial towns were far away, a smudge of smoke and misery hidden by the curve of the earth's surface'.[2] Finance industry and much of the non-unionised working class might have not been so well served by Conservative policies but nevertheless had preferred the pieties of Baldwin to the spectres of socialism and trade unionism. An election in 1940 would have confirmed this dominance but Conservative certainties were destroyed by the fall of Chamberlain, the entry of senior Labour figures into the Churchill coalition and the Dunkirk evacuation. Many of the traditional political class were condemned as incompetent and by implication anti-patriotic. *Guilty Men* and *The Lion and the Unicorn* articulated the sentiments of a radical if politically ambiguous shift. At the level of daily experience the change was powered by geographical mobility the growth of effective trade unionism, especially in southern England, and the mass entry of women into the labour market.

In 1945 Labour's support amongst the working-class electorate grew dramatically especially in Birmingham and much of southern England. The party had broken out of the unionised and often occupationally specific sections of the working class that had provided the basis for its decisive parliamentary entry in 1922. Whether Labour made a significant advance within the middle class in 1945 is debatable. Probably a minority of largely younger middle-class voters often removed temporarily from familiar environments backed Labour. The Conservatives continued to poll strongly across much of rural and small-town England and in many suburbs. Some wartime experiences such as the impact of urban working-class evacuees on rural communities could confirm long-held prejudices. For some, defeat did not shatter old categories. A woman dining at the Savoy allegedly responded 'But this is terrible—*they've* elected a Labour government and *the country* will never stand for that' (p.76). The Labour landslide perhaps demonstrated a decline in deference or at least in the rituals of deference. 'My man', called out a blazered, straw-hatted 14-year-old public schoolboy, John Rae, as he stood with his trunk on the station platform at Bishop Stortford that late July. 'No' came the porter's quiet but firm reply, 'that sort of thing is all over now.' (p.80). Certainly one sort of thing was all over. The electoral coalition that had given the Conservatives their pre-war dominance had been fractured.

Kynaston recalls how when the new Commons met for the first time Churchill was greeted by his backbenchers with a 'For he's a jolly good fellow'. The Labour benches responded by singing 'the Red Flag'. The initiator was supposedly George Griffiths a Yorkshire miners' MP. Kynaston sees this overture as deceptive. 'Griffiths may have got them singing, but it was the lawyers, teachers, journalists, doctors, managers and technicians who would principally be calling the tune' (p.82). He notes that after the 1945 election only 38 per cent of Labour MPs came from a working-class background compared with 72 per cent after the 1935 election. Yet background is an ambiguous term. Does it refer to MPs' occupations prior to their election or to those of their parents? The contrast between 1935 and 1945 also reflects the tendency for trade-union sponsored MPs to be concentrated in the safer seats.

Amongst Labour's 'Big Five' Attlee (Haileybury and Oxford) Dalton (Eton and Cambridge) and Cripps (Winchester and London) were joined by Bevin (Bristol casual labour market) and Morrison (London retail trade). Such distinctions illuminate significant identities within Labour culture but of themselves offer little insight into which tunes were called and why. Leading figures were often sensitive to the need to harmonise ministerial, party and trade-union concerns. Attlee perhaps idealised working-class common sense as represented by some cabinet colleagues. Concern with harmonisation had been deepened by authorised understandings of the 1931 disaster that had shaped the politics of this generation of Labour leaders. Never again must a Labour government be wrecked on a conflict between some senior ministers and leading figures within the Trades' Union Congress. The Attlee Government consulted carefully with the TUC on matters of common concern. Kynaston notes the TUC's reluctant acquiescence in a wages' policy early in 1948 (pp.229–30). The language of 'calling the tune' and of dominance is inappropriate for such a complex relationship. The theme can be examined further by looking at the ambiguities of one of the Attlee Government's most symbolic measures the nationalisation of the coal industry.

Kynaston expresses scepticism as to whether the majority of workers in the designated industries were enthusiasts for nationalisation (p.141). He cites a source claiming that the workforce at a south Yorkshire colliery was evenly divided. The source is a colliery managing director. That managing directors made such claims is part of the political texture of 1946; that such a claim can be presented as evidence of worker scepticism is questionable. Voices need context otherwise there is a tendency for a contemporary and partisan assessment to surreptitiously achieve authorial status.

Similarly the portrait of Emmanuel Shinwell the responsible cabinet minister is debatable. His failure during the 1947 fuel crisis is indisputable but Kynaston's characterisation of him as left wing (p.189) is misleading. Shinwell's socialist rhetoric was reserved for high days and holidays. During his early parliamentary career he had been a vigorous supporter of Ramsay MacDonald. Backed by the Durham Miners' Association he had gained credibility by destroying his former patron at the 1935 Seaham election. Subsequently he refused junior office in the Churchill Coalition. Instead as one of its backbench critics he had acquired a deceptively iconoclastic status. To cite his junior minister and successor Hugh Gaitskell on the harassed Shinwell's shortcomings is problematic. As a Wykehamist and a Whitehall insider Gaitskell was not the most empathetic observer. He was close to Dalton who was a violent critic of Shinwell. More generally Gaitskell's diary understandably expresses his political and social prejudices. The problem with Kynaston's method of multiple voices is that such expressions can be elevated to considered judgments.

Kynaston addresses the question of support for coal nationalisation by distinguishing the expectations of miners from the programme of their union. 'Did the rank and file as opposed to some leaders and activists truly see nationalisation as ushering in either actually or potentially fundamental changes in working conditions and employer/employee relationships?' (p.187). As elsewhere Kynaston necessarily rests his argument on selected secondary sources. These include the contemporary research carried out by Ferdynand Zweig and retrospective interviews conducted by Zweiniger-Bargielowska in South Wales and Ackers and Payne in the Midlands.[3] Zweiniger-Bargielowska found miners in supposedly radical South Wales retrospectively emphasising their concern with pay and conditions and claiming that they had had little interest in the wider organisation of the industry. The Midlands material is coloured by pre-1947 patterns of employer paternalism and industrial harmony. The variety of expectation contrasts with the uniformity of party and trade-union agendas and of some scholarly writing. The emphasis on diversity is at one with Kynaston's overall approach.

Subsequently he offers a more exacting standard. 'Overall a range of expectations and non-expectations obtained at the start of 1947 but few miners seemed to equate nationalisation with workers' control whatever that might mean' (p.188). The criterion arguably marginalises context. Labour Party–TUC policymaking between the wars had effectively ruled out any possibility of workers' control. The public corporation model would be the paradigm for the Attlee Government's nationalisation programme.

Ministers and officials hailed the early success of the nationalised coal industry but Zweig found hostility to bureaucracy and to allegedly highly paid officials who contributed little (p.203). The disenchantment seemed to be demonstrated in the increasing incidence of unofficial disputes most famously the Yorkshire strike in the summer of 1947. Zweig insisted that miners were disillusioned about the experience of nationalisation. As a contemporary quip had it, at least old King Cole knew how many fiddlers he had.

Kynaston is generally sympathetic to Zweig's work but notes that a claim of disillusion necessitates 'illusions in the first place about the fundamental reordering of social and industrial relations' (p.203). Against this vision Kynaston juxtaposes more modest aspirations for 'solid unglamorous incremental improvements' and suggests reasonably that these were beginning to be met. Why should these be alternatives? Zweig's respondents endorsed the incremental changes but wanted more. Union leaderships in the left inclined coalfields most notably Scotland and South Wales pursued such targets but remained in some sense committed to a more thorough transformation of the industry and the wider society. That aspiration need not be attached to the elusive notion of workers' control.

Beyond the specific debate Kynaston raises an important historiographical question. In part the criteria for assessing coal nationalisation depend on 'how one sees the miners'. He highlights one view characteristic of the 1970s and strengthened by the strikes of 1972 and 1974—'that they were natural militants who wanted workers' control and had been cruelly betrayed by the stodgy bureaucratic form that public ownership took' (p.204). But there are no natural militants. If by the 1970s there had been a betrayal that had facilitated some radicalisation this was much more the consequence of mass closures forced migration and a relative deterioration in wages. Such disillusion was strengthened by the generalised discontent that had followed the introduction of the National Power Loading Agreement from 1966. It nevertheless required creative leadership to achieve collective expression. Kynaston contrasts the naïve image of *natural* militants with what he presents as a more plausible basis for a narrative. Miners not only exhibited class solidarity and physical courage. They were real and therefore flawed people, 'conservative (including about such matters as Polish labour and new forms of mechanisation), usually money minded, sometimes bloody minded, always deeply mistrustful' (p.204). This does not rule out the radicalism of real people.

The profile can be extended. Apparent class solidarity was often occupational solidarity. Even this could be brittle as between coalfields communities and even grades in the same pit. More fundamentally assessment of alternatives is not just a matter of 'how one sees the miners' but of how they viewed their choices. To seek what seemed feasible and yet to wish for more thorough but unlikely changes could rest on a reasoned assessment of opportunities and constraints not least the obstacles to effective collective action. The public culture of a Durham mining community was sketched by an observer during the 1951 election. It suggests that at this local level official and private understandings were not too far apart.

> Nearly all the speakers were local men active in the trade unions, local government or the mines. They came and talked of the past, of the part they themselves had played in the bitter struggles against poverty and unemployment in the area, of men and events already known to their audiences. They spoke always with feeling and sometimes with anger: above all they spoke only of what they knew.[4]

Some of the book's most powerful sections convey the experience of work in the pits on the docks and in the car industry. The last gives a compelling sense of contrasting production methods and managerial and workers' cultures between Dagenham, Luton, Cowley, Coventry and Longbridge. The Cowley material offers an insight into the character and limits of war-time and post-war radicalism. Returning ex-servicemen had no time for the old order. They wanted a shift 'away from the hire and fire and the chargehands' pets, the men who came in regularly with the bag of garden products which they left by the chargehands' desks' (p.491).

In Coventry the Standard managing director Sir John Black negotiated a high wage high output policy with the Transport and General Workers' district secretary Jack Jones. Unions effectively hired labour. Piece rates were negotiated with fifteen workplace gangs. Across the Coventry car plants the monotony of the tracks was balanced with a culture of autonomy which was based not on substantive skills but on work gang solidarity with the pattern of work collectively determined by the workers within the limits laid down by managers.

Kynaston's account and characterisation owe much to work by Paul Thompson.[5] This not only recreated the world of the Coventry car makers but made a comparison with their counterparts in Turin. The comparison raises issues central to the overall British experience. Thompson insisted that the Turin car workers and the Italian Communist Party had drawn a sharp lesson from their experiences of fascism, recession and military defeat. The permanence of the industrial economy could not be taken for granted. Post-war reconstruction could not be just social. It must also be economic. The Italian vision involved a commitment to technological advance as necessary for social progress. Perhaps the presentation of the Italian Communist Party and Italian trade unions is idealised but here at least is a standard for assessment of the British experience that is more rigorous than references to workers' control. In contrast Thompson claims that Britain's early industrialisation produced a pre-socialist trade unionism that retained craft residues and restricted itself to pragmatic political interventions. In addition Thompson emphasised the complacency of British nationalism an imperial nation that had just been on the winning side in a global conflict. The stifling impact of Great Power ambitions is recurrent in Kynaston's text but typically on international and colonial issues (for example, p.135).

Kynaston's presentation of the Coventry case is supportive of a broader theme within his work the impact of trade unions as barriers to modernisation. His reference point is Allan Flanders's commendation of the voluntarist system of industrial relations.[6] This

> was imbued with the assumption that enhanced trade-union power was, if exercised in the appropriate way, an almost unequivocal social and economic good. The appropriate way included moderation in recourse to the strike weapon; the use wherever possible of industry-wide collective bargaining; and such bargaining to be reliant upon long-nurtured codes rather than externally imposed legal contracts (p.455).

Kynaston suggests three critical weaknesses in this instrument for progress. One is uncontroversial, the gender imbalance in trade-union membership at least in part a consequence of the hostility of male trade unionists to gender equality in the workplace or indeed to women as industrial workers in peacetime. Trade unions were often at one with the expectations and prejudices of the wider society but were in a weak position to respond to future changes in employment patterns. More controversially Kynaston emphasises the gap between leaders and members. Insofar as his point concerns the marginality of the union for many members this was not a post war novelty despite romanticism about an allegedly more participatory past.[7] Another emphasis concerns the rise of shop stewards and the possible subversion of national agreements. This raises complex issues about members' preferences and devolved democracy allied to the possibility that Flanders's vision necessitated a relatively passive membership whose consent could be delivered for settlements agreed by national officials.

Most significantly Kynaston spotlights the economism of the unions, a theme that connects to Thompson's Coventry–Turin comparison. He suggests a narrowness of outlook that blocked any willingness to innovate, or to quote one of his favourite sources Zweig: 'the union is the greatest bulwark of industrial conservatism'.[8] The diagnosis licenses a characterisation and a putative future.

> The question was whether, given the Labour government's natural reluctance to jeopardise its social contract with organised labour, a future government of a different hue would have the resolve to put industrial relations on a more flexible and productive basis (p.467).

Here is a theme for future volumes. There is a hint of a later debate about the extent to which the Labour Party was critically flawed as an instrument of progress because of its close relationship with the unions. In the context of *Austerity Britain* the characterisation ignores the extent to which the fact of a Labour government scrupulously implementing its domestic agenda modified trade-union behaviour not least over wages.

When the porter at Bishop Stortford insisted 'that sort of thing is all over now' his assessment would prove valid in the workplace. Continuing full employment and the exorcism of insecurity are insufficiently emphasised by Kynaston. They could seem for many, more than enough to compensate for the shortages that he chronicles so vividly. Recent emphases on the postwar politics of consumption have been indispensable not least in balancing the masculine bias of workplace studies.[9] Yet this emphasis needs in turn to be balanced against the belief held by many that the government should be given the credit for workers' greater sense of security. It is in this context that the Labour votes of 1950 and 1951 must be placed.

Yet the end to 'that sort of thing' was very restricted. Beyond full employment, welfare and the public sector little changed. Pre-war rituals of the upper and middle classes quickly revived. Orwell's wartime fantasy of the red militias billeted at the Ritz remained precisely that.[10] The Attlee government might in its first months have faced a demoralised opposition but any space for early radicalism was invaded by immediate crises. The abrupt termination of Lend Lease, the threat of national bankruptcy and the rigorous conditions of the American loan were challenge enough. More basically Labour's agenda for change was focussed on a narrow range of economic and social issues. Party and TUC policymaking in the 1930s had expressed these priorities. In many respects the government's narrow focus on jobs welfare and decent housing might have been at one with the expectations of its core support. If ministers believed that their fulfilment would produce cultural and ethical change they were mistaken.

Beyond the government's priorities stand the complexities of the Cold War and the extent to which they limited the government's options. Kynaston focuses on the consequences of international polarisation for British experiences—the discrimination against communists in some employment sectors from 1948, Ministerial and press insistence that strikes were Communist inspired and the impact of the Korean war on the economy and on the government's stability.[11]

The focus is valuable but the execution is problematic. His insistence that the government's anti-communism did not necessarily occupy the moral low ground claims a vantage point that seems at variance with his treatment of trade unionism. He insists that in assessing Cold War politics context is everything and cites Alan Bullock's conclusion to his biography of Ernest Bevin in support. 'There was a real danger of the Soviet Union and other communists taking advantage of the weakness of Western Europe to extend their power. We know that this did not follow but nobody knew it at the time'.[12]

This argument is loose. It combines unsubstantiated claims about Soviet intentions and capabilities with an assertion about what was known (or perhaps believed would be the more appropriate word), at the time. Unlike in the analysis of government trade-union relations counterfactuals remain unexplored. If context is vital this maxim must apply in every case.

A great strength of Kynaston's work comes with the richness and ambiguity of its many voices. British communists are rarely accorded such variety. At its worst their characterisation collapses into Cold War stereotypes. There are orthodox party sentiments from Lawrence Daly, images of east European Utopia from Willie Gallacher's *The Case for Communism* and E.P. Thompson's recollection of the freezing of post-war party life. But Thompson's explanation of this Cold War deterioration was characteristically nuanced. Recent scholarly work on the prosopography of British Communism should have shattered the credibility of older caricatures.[13]

Kynaston's stereotypes sometimes extend more broadly across the left. Occasionally he cannot resist a cheap shot.

In April (1949) the shelling by Communist forces of British ships on the Yangtse, together with the heroic if bloody escape of *HMS Amethyst* into the open sea, seems to have struck a deeply patriotic chord in the working-class breast. But as so often Labour's intellectuals did not get it. 'British warships' Richard Crossman (Winchester-Oxford undergraduate-Oxford don-people's tribune) declared in the *Sunday Pictorial* 'are as out of place on the Yangtse as Chinese warships would be on the Thames'. (pp.341–2).

But who did not get it? The *Boy's Own* appeal of the *Amethyst*'s heroic escape is obvious as is the fact that the whole episode stemmed from the residual and by 1949 doomed colonialism of British merchants in southern China.[14] Kynaston acknowledges the non-affordability of Britain's Great Power status. He emphasises working-class economism and complacency about the pre-eminence of the British economy. But a patriotism based on unrealistic assumptions about the affordability of a world role becomes a means for exposing the unrepresentative sentiments of left intellectuals.

The book's political climax comes with the cabinet resignations of Aneurin Bevan and Harold Wilson in April 1951. The exploration of this crisis is effectively interwoven with a kaleidoscope of images. The book ends not with Bevan's departure to the back benches but with Blackpool and Stanley Mathews losing their second post-war cup final. This Geordie triumph shows Kynaston at his eloquent best. In contrast the treatment of Bevan shows the problems with his method. Bevan is presented through the images of his critics. Sir Raymond Streat, chairman of the Cotton Board, writes of his fear at hearing Bevan insist on steel nationalisation—'a void where there are no morals, no faiths, no loves' (p.535). All Bevan had done was to insist hyperbolically that the measure was essential to preserve Labour's soul. At the first post-election cabinet meeting in March 1950 Patrick Gordon Walker recorded an hostile portrait of Bevan. 'Bevan was very isolated and unpopular. MPs and Ministers seem to be strongly against Bevan' (pp.535–6). Gordon Walker was a close ally of Morrison, Bevan's principal opponent on steel nationalisation and hardly an objective witness. He recorded Bevan as alone in his insistence that the government with its minuscule majority push forward with steel nationalisation. Yet Bevan won on steel. Kynaston does not explain this outcome. Clearly his source did not present the full picture. Gaitskell's diary entries present Bevan as the unstable Welsh individualist capable of creative and brilliant initiatives but a poor team player, a blend of stereotype and half truth. Gaitskell like Gordon Walker was hardly an impartial witness but rather a tough factional politician, quietly ambitious and adept at courting influential figures within the labour movement. Kynaston's account offers limited understanding of Bevan's appeal. No voices speak on his behalf.[15] Equally there is no serious attempt to understand how Bevan felt when he was not chosen by Attlee to succeed either Cripps at the Treasury or Bevin at the Foreign Office. After all he was the minister viewed widely as the architect of the government's most significant achievement. Kynaston's voices in this instance do not produce a credible conversation.

Bevan would present the factional struggles that would mark the Labour Party for a generation as not least about Labour's identity and authenticity, the choice between a product of Winchester and New College and a miner's son from Tredegar. Yet Labour identities were never that dichotomous. Deference flourished alongside egalitarianism, pragmatic respectability coupled with romantic rebellion.

Labour's sentiments on education and social mobility were ambiguous. Education had been a concern of the pre-war party but the Churchill Coalition laid down the pattern of post-war educational opportunity in the 1944 Act. The consequence was the continuation of a selective system that was loaded heavily against working-class children, but whose underlying assumptions few Labour politicians questioned. Selection was at one with the dominant views of the psychologist Sir Cyril Burt. He had been influenced heavily by the eugenics movement and proclaimed that intelligence could be tested scientifically and that its level was primarily the result of hereditary factors. Burt's claims could not only legitimise selection at 11 years old but within the grammar schools could support further streaming within the chosen minority. The small number of working-class children who entered grammar schools faced socialisation into a world of academic competition and petty snobberies, not least for boys the division of games into approved and non-approved. One of Kynaston's Tory sources Kenneth Preston taught English at Keighley Grammar School. He noted with relief the start of the 1951 Easter holiday. 'The School has had the usual exhortation from Head about not watching football matches' (p.568). Some rebelled against the rigours and the bigotries. Others endorsed them. The culture of the grammar school distanced them from their neighbourhoods. It shaped their images of social classes and of merit and desert.

Brian Jackson and Dennis Marsden charted the experiences of 88 working-class scholarship children from Huddersfield. Their educational and social journeys did not necessarily engender empathy with those whom they had left behind.

> I'm glad to get out of the working class. I should say by and large that the working class are those that lack abilities, those who can't get on, that's who they are…the *Mirror* people, the dead beats. You read about these

miners, and you hear about them getting £20 or £30 a week. And they can hardly write their names.[16]

The Attlee Government had administered the 1944 Act. The outcome was a limited mobility that in its prejudices and taboos facilitated the perpetuation of 'that sort of thing'.

I read Jackson and Marsden in the sixth form of my boys'-only, rugby-playing, grammar school. They offered evidence and argument to place alongside my barely articulated feelings. I understood the book as an indictment of Macmillan's Britain whereas the research really highlighted the limited radicalism of the 1940. The misunderstanding was perhaps intelligible. Sir Alec Douglas Home a recently arrived and unexpected prime minister was challenged by Wilsonian meritocracy wrapped in radical rhetoric. In those months that preceded the 1964 election another 1945 seemed possible. But memories of Labour's earlier triumph and of the years that followed were both selective and contested. Whatever the merits of Kynaston's specific arguments his great strength is to emphasise the complexity and ambiguity of our memories and of the diverse ways that some understandings of the past become codified into authorised versions.

David Howell
University of York

Notes

1. For the transcript of the Laski trial see *The Laski Libel Action Verbatim Report* (London *n.d.*). See also David Howell 'The Laski Libel Trial' in Keith Gildart, David Howell and Neville Kirk (eds) *Dictionary of Labour Biography volume 11* (London, 2003).
2. George Orwell *Homage to Catalonia* (Harmondsworth, 1974), p.221.
3. Ferdynand Zweig, *Men in the Pits* (London 1948); Ina Zweiniger-Bargielowska, 'South Wales Miners' Attitudes towards Nationalisation: an essay in oral history', *Llafur*, 6 (1994), pp.70–84; Peter Ackers and Jonathan Payne, 'Before the Storm: the experience of nationalization and the proposals for industrial relations partnership in the British coal industry 1947–1972—rethinking the militant narrative', *Social History*, 27 (2002), pp184–209.
4. E.W. Hughes in David Butler, *The British General Election of 1951* (London, 1952), p.153.
5. Paul Thompson, 'Playing at Being Skilled Men: factory culture and pride in work skills among Coventry car workers', *Social History*, 13 (1988), pp.45–69.
6. See Allan Flanders, *Trade Unions* (London, 1952).
7. For a contemporary study see Joseph Goldstein, *The Government of British Trade*

Unions. A Study of Apathy and the Democratic Process in the Transport and General Workers' Union (London, 1952).
8. Ferdynand Zweig, *The British Worker* (London, 1952), p.175.
9. Ina Zweiniger-Bargielowska, *Austerity in Britain. Rationing, Controls and Consumption 1939–1955* (Oxford 2000).
10. George Orwell 'My Country Right or Left' in *The Collected Essays, Journalism and Letters of George Orwell Volume 1: An Age Like This 1920–1940* (Harmondsworth, 1975), p.591.
11. Kynaston notes anti-Communist characterisations of strikes at pp.340–1 and pp.478–85 and provides evidence that disaffection in the docks had more local causes. For an analysis of the 1949 London dock strike widely presented not least by the government as Communist inspired see Peter Weiler, *British Labour and the Cold War* (Stanford, 1988), chapter 7.
12. Alan Bullock, *Ernest Bevin Foreign Secretary 1945–1951* (Oxford, 1985), p.845.
13. Kevin Morgan Gidon Cohen and Andrew Flinn, *Communists and British Society 1920–1991* (London, 2007).
14. For a judicious account of the affair see the entry on the hero of the *Amethyst*'s escape J. S. Kerans in the *Oxford Dictionary of National Biography Volume 31* (Oxford 2004), pp.397–401 by Malcolm H. Murfett. Kerans was later Conservative MP for The Hartlepools 1959–64.
15. For an eloquent defence see Dai Smith, *Aneurin Bevan and the World of South Wales* (Cardiff, 1993).
16. Brian Jackson and Dennis Marsden, *Education and the Working Class* (London, 1962) pp.204–5.

C. Alexander McKinley. *Illegitimate Children of the Enlightenment: Anarchists and the French Revolution, 1880–1914* (Peter Lang, New York, 2008), ISBN 978–1–4331–0059–8, 237pp., £35.50.

Whilst for certain Chinese communists the mid-twentieth century may have been too early to pass judgment on the legacy of the French Revolution, for anarchists in the Third Republic the lessons of 1789 were far clearer. Yet as McKinley's book emphasises, the anarchists were far from alone in interpreting the Revolution as an affirmation of their politics. 'Moderate republicans, like Jules Ferry and the Opportunists', 'Gambetta and his followers' and 'radicals' like the historian Alphonse Aulard, all saw an understanding of the Revolution as a source of political legitimacy in the volatile opening years of the Third Republic. Throw into this mix figures like Blanqui, Clemenceau, Jean Jaurès and Guesde, and it becomes apparent that these lessons remained very much up for grabs, as well as revealing the pervasiveness of the Revolution in French political culture one hundred years on (pp.7, 73).

In this vibrant political milieu it might be thought, given its comparative marginality, that the anarchist movement's claims to the Revolutionary legacy may have been more optimistic than others. After all, the prevailing image of Jacobin violence clashes with the libertarian ethos of anarchist politics, even though anarchism was also to acquire a sanguinary reputation in the course of the nineteenth century. Yet, McKinley makes forceful claims for the centrality of an understanding of the French Revolution to the wider anarchist project. A variety of anarchist intellectuals and groups, notably the anarchist-communist Peter Kropotkin and syndicalist Emile Pouget, attempted to elaborate a different conception of the Revolution, and ultimately resurrect it as a model for future struggle.

These interventions allowed the burgeoning anarchist movement to associate itself with the myths of the Revolution; revealing anarchist tactics in action, and offering a valuable degree of authenticity. At the same time the anarchists were able to distinguish themselves from competing political movements that also saw themselves as heirs to the traditions of Revolutionary France. 'Whilst Marxists like Jaurès and Guesde might see the Revolution as the triumph of the middle class over their aristocratic predecessors', or the 'conservative Republic' might stress 'the ideas of republican liberty and the legitimacy of popular sovereignty' above armed uprising, the anarchists saw the Revolution as an epitome of their own belief in the dynamism and self-sufficiency of a rebellious populace (pp.14, 169). The Revolution offered the anarchists an opportunity to critique both of these positions. Thus, Kropotkin suggested that the Marxist notion of dictatorship of the proletariat derived from the 'same statist school as the Jacobins' and would ultimately drown the revolution in blood, and condemned the selective memory of contemporary Republicans in their commemoration of the Revolution as a nationalist event, not class war (pp.72, 170).

These themes are explored in *Illegitimate Children of the Enlightenment*. The first three chapters present a broad, intellectual history of *fin-de-siècle* anarchist writing on the Revolution, including an ambitious exploration of the relationship between the *philosophes* of Revolution (Voltaire, Rousseau and Diderot) and anarchism. The final chapters present more of a cultural history, exploring the symbols of popular culture, public commemoration, and the anarchist reaction to these.

As McKinley notes: 'It is difficult to speak…of [a] systemised school of anarchist thought…during the Third Republic'. He, therefore focusses on the 'crucial' schools of 'anarchist theory…anarcho-communists and anarcho-syndicalists' (p.83). While this pragmatic move is understandable, the relationship between anarchist–communism and syndicalism is somewhat underdeveloped, and the 'anarcho–individualists', a group apparently 'as much cultural as political', are quickly dismissed (p.84). Given the complexity of even defining the term anarchism this is a minor point, and it is a justifiable conclusion that the 'social' varieties of anarchism (mutualist, collectivist, communist, syndicalist) have historically tended to exercise the greatest influence.[1] It is, however, a weakness shared by many histories of anarchism that tend to leave these labels uncontested.

The argument developed across the first two chapters is that the anarchist narrative of the revolution, expounded primarily by Kropotkin, Pouget and Jean Grave, was based upon both a 'positive position' and 'a number of mistakes...to be avoided.' The positive position is identified as comprising three points, aspects of a wider anarchist doctrine: the role of the 'people', including 'peasants in the countryside or the *sans-culottes* in Paris', the *enragés* as an example of a revolutionary minority, and a view of the Revolution as challenging the social and economic bases of the *ancien regime* (p.13). Kropotkin is unsurprisingly a pervasive presence, as the most famous and systematic anarchist propagandist of the period. A key emphasis, developed in his writing on the Revolution over something of a *longue durée*, is the presence of a 'revolutionary spirit' amongst the French peasantry, allegedly evidenced by the frequency of *jacqueries*. As Kropotkin and Grave's paper *La Révolte* concluded, it was the popular initiative that forced the destruction of feudalism, not the activity of enlightened representatives:

Profitant de l'effervescence générale et de la désorganisation du pouvoir, ils se mirent eux-mêmes à brûler les châteaux, à détuire les terriers et forcer les seigneurs à abdiquer leurs droits.

Rather than a story of the *grande hommes* of the Revolution, the anarchists saw the localism of the peasantry as the motor of revolutionary change. The conclusion being that the Convention 'did not do more than give its sanction to what the peasants had already accomplished.'[2]

The next chapter on the relationship between Enlightenment and anarchist philosophy follows a similar course, by tracing how various anarchists attempted to gain legitimacy by associating their political beliefs with the intellectual traditions of revolutionary France. Voltaire, Rousseau and Diderot were all incorporated at times into the anarchist canon, although as becomes clear, there was far from universal agreement on this. Even Rousseau, the most commonly referenced *philosophe* by anarchist writers, could be denounced by Bakunin as possessing the 'falsest mind...of the last century.'[3] McKinley argues that, whilst it has become common to include Rousseau as a precursor of anarchism, a 'detailed analysis to support this conclusion' is often absent (p.92). To address this, aspects of Rousseau's philosophy most relevant in relation to anarchist politics are explored: 'the state of nature and man's natural goodness, the corruption of modern society, private property, the social contract, the rule of law, civil religion, direct democracy, and the role of education' (p.95). The conclusion, unsurprisingly for a figure variously seen as the father of totalitarianism and anarchism, is that this legacy remains ambiguous, even if the anarchists tended to appropriate 'the ideas of Rousseau to fit their needs' (p.105).

The book is most engaging when discussing the 'popular culture' of the Revolution; the 'visual images' and songs described in the penultimate chapter, and the relationship with Bastille Day, which closes the book. Central to these posters and cartoons was the reiteration of the 'chain of continuity' between the Revolution and anarchist politics, which was clear in the more theoretical discussions (p.119). The violence of these images is particularly striking, with the hanging of landlords a recurring feature. Rather than the guillotine, dismissed as a symbol of Jacobin (and therefore 'statist') violence, the representation of mob justice reflects the anarchist notion of the 'people' as the driving force of the Revolution (p.140). The guillotine remained the method of execution in the Third Republic, as Ravachol discovered in 1892, and was unsurprisingly condemned. The rich tradition of songs associated with the Revolution, a popular modern historical source, similarly reflects this anarchist sensitivity to traditions incorporated by the state. Thus, *la Marseillaise* fluctuated in popularity, losing its prestige as it became increasingly associated with militarism, and *Ça Ira* and *La Carmagnole*, proved most popular, given their connection to 'the most radical events of the…Revolution' (p.141).

Just as popular radicalism was emphasised in the anarchists' choice of songs, this was mirrored in their relationship with Bastille Day. If the 'conservative Republic' preferred to look to the *Fête de la Fédération* as a symbol of 'patriotic unity', the anarchists instead looked to the dynamism of the people expressed in their version of the storming of the Bastille (p.168). July 14 was thus a symbol of class war, a demonstration of what the liberated instincts of the mass could achieve, and each anniversary a fresh opportunity for direct action. It was, above all, an affirmation of Danton's frequently quoted rallying call: '*De l'audace, encore de l'audace, toujours de l'audace!*' (p.187).

McKinley's book suggests that perhaps the legacy of the French Revolution is more contentious that might be first thought. It offers a useful exploration of *fin-de-siècle* anarchism, supported by formidable primary research, though it does contain some weaknesses. The relationship between anarchism and Enlightenment philosophy is a vast and complex problem, and the limited space afforded to it cannot do it justice. There is also a tendency to over-emphasise the anarchist fascination with violence. This seems justified in much of McKinley's discussion, but given the frequent invocation of Kropotkin's work, it is perhaps as well to remember the often deep ambivalence of anarchists like Kropotkin concerning the role of violence in any future revolution. Finally, and admittedly a minor quibble, the book could have done with more attentive proofreading, with the regular typographical mistakes and repetitious phrases detracting from the interesting research that has been done.

Matthew S. Adams
University of Manchester

Notes

1. Consider: Michael Freeden, *Ideologies and Political Theory: A Conceptual Approach* (Oxford, 2004), p.311; David Miller, *Anarchism* (London, 1984); Daniel Guérin, *Anarchism: From Theory to Practice*, Mary Klopper (trans) (New York, 1970), pp.9–34.
2. Peter Kropotkin, 'Local Action' [1887] in Nicolas Walter and Heiner Becker (eds), *Act for Yourselves: Articles from Freedom 1886–1907* (London, 1998), p.42.
3. Michael Bakunin, *God and the State* (New York, 1970 [1916]), p.79.

Wendy Z. Goldman, **Terror and Democracy in the Age of Stalin: The Social Dynamics of Repression** (Cambridge University Press, Cambridge, 2007), ISBN 978–0–521–86614–9, x+274pp., £40.00 (hb)

Wendy Goldman's latest book is a departure from her previous two monographs which concentrated on women's experiences in the Soviet Union. Yet Goldman has brought to this subject the excellent qualities of her earlier works: the exhaustive use of archival materials, the commitment to allowing the people's voices to be heard and the determination to explore the 'mechanics' of a particular phenomenon.

As the introduction to *Terror and Democracy* demonstrates the Soviet Great Terror of the 1930s is a tangled subject which the opening of the archives has complicated, rather than simplified. Old assumptions about the numbers of victims of the Terror have been challenged and new questions about the popular response to, and involvement in, the purges have been raised. It is to this latter area of research that *Terror and Democracy* contributes by using Soviet unions and factory party committees as illuminating case studies. Goldman traces the gradual shift in worker attitudes towards the existence of enemies in the Soviet Union from apathy, during the early trials connected to Kirov's murder, to enthusiasm for the exposure and arrest of enemies in their midst, and then to panic as workers began to realise that anyone could be denounced. According to Goldman, this change of heart can be explained by the way in which the *portrayal* of enemies changed over time, making the existence of enemies relevant to the workers. Between 1934 and 1938 the threat shifted from groups of politicians plotting to overthrow Stalin and the government, to groups of local party or union members planning to harm workers by sabotaging factories. Most importantly, this new enemy was a perfect scapegoat for the workers' frustration, anger and despair at the appalling living and working conditions they had had to endure since the start of the first Five-Year Plan. It is not made clear to what extent the identification of enemies as 'wreckers' was a conscious or cynical act by the government. At times it seems that it was simply another fabrication in the show trials, at others that it was a deliberate addition to the charges against former oppositionists so that workers would be distracted from their genuine complaints and drawn into the struggle against enemies. In either case, the result was that where the party and government had previously been blamed for the workers' suffering, now individuals in communities, who were familiar faces, were criticised and denounced.

Central to Goldman's work is her assertion that democracy and repression were linked and that the former was vital for the expansion of the latter. She argues that the party genuinely sought to reintroduce democracy to the unions in the mid-1930s as a way of encouraging the workers to embrace the destruction of enemies more fully. During 1937, elections with secret ballots and without candidate lists were held in every union committee and high numbers of representatives were replaced. In a rare moment of empowerment, workers were able to denounce the committee members they were voting out and scrutinise those they were voting in. Often the new representatives were also subjected to denunciations (and NKVD investigations). Goldman also shows, however, that the efforts at democratisation were doomed to failure in the poisonous atmosphere of the 1930s, not least because of the party's dubious motives for beginning them in the first place, that is as a means to root out enemies. Democratic elections did not solve many of the problems workers hoped they would: high-level union representatives were often able to move laterally (even if voted out), party members continued to dominate committees and those who were democratically elected often proved to be incapable of improving the workers' lot, both through their own incompetence and corruption, and because of the lack of resources and support from above. Last, because democratisation was directly linked to the intensification of the terror, as the repression eased off, so the need for democracy reduced and the party reverted to engineering appointments to union and committee positions.

The greatest strength of this book is Goldman's intensive archival research, which is made easily accessible to the reader by the use of footnotes, rather than endnotes. In particular, the use of stenographic records of worker, union and party meetings provide rich detail about what workers thought and how they responded to events, as well as to different types of 'enemy'. The heavy use of direct quotation in *Terror and Democracy* illustrates vividly the changing content and form of workers' complaints. The reader can also observe individuals' growing confidence in making denunciations and later their rising panic as arrests became more frequent and less predictable. It is praiseworthy that women's voices, so often lost in the narrative of the Great Terror, are included, both amongst the accused and the accusers.

The dominance of 'voices' in the book serves to highlight how little communication actually occurred between the government and the workers during the terror. At the top all cried out for the exposure of political enemies, insisting on the existence of vast conspiracies. Meanwhile workers attempted to tell their leaders about their horrendous living and working conditions, but had to use the vocabulary of 'wrecking' and sabotage to be taken seriously. Caught between the two, Goldman shows, were the local union representatives, and regional party leaders, who were attacked from both sides, and condemned for a combination of alleged political failings, real economic problems beyond their control, and difficulties caused by their own negligence. They in turn blamed their superiors and sought out yet more enemies.

Goldman traces the pattern of denunciation and counter-denunciation to the climax of the terror where everyone felt they must attack another, in order to avoid being attacked themselves, where, as she puts it, the snake 'devouring its tail, reached the point where its mouth swallowed its head' (p.252). She concludes with the observation that repressive measures against workers intensified further after 1938, even though the terror itself had subsided.

In *Dr Zhivago*, Pasternak writes about the 'inhuman power of the lie' dominating the Soviet Union in the 1930s. Goldman demonstrates that a more complicated relationship between the truth and lies existed, and it was in part due to the fatal combination of the two that the period proved so destructive. *Terror and Democracy* highlights above all that if an honest, open dialogue about the harsh realities of industrialisation could have been established between the party, the unions and the workers, without discussions having to be cloaked in a political witch-hunt, a vast deal of suffering could have been avoided.

Katy Turton
Queen's Universitiy, Belfast

Socialist History Society

The **Socialist History Society** was founded in 1992. Its members include many of Britain's leading socialist and labour historians, both academic and amateur.

The **SHS** holds regular events, public meetings and one-off conferences, and contributes to current historical debates and controversies.

The society produces a range of publications, including the journal *Socialist History*. It can sometimes assist with individual student research.

The **SHS** is the successor to the Communist Party History Group, established in 1946.

The Society is now entirely independent of all political parties and groups. It is engaged in, and seeks to encourage, historical studies from a Marxist and broadly defined left perspective. It is concerned with every aspect of human history from early social formations to the present day. It is particularly interested in the struggles of labour, women, progressive and peace movements throughout the world, as well as the movements and achievements of colonial peoples, black people, and other oppressed communities in seeking justice, human dignity and liberation.

Each year the **SHS** produces two issues of the journal *Socialist History*, one or two historical pamphlets inthe *Occasional Papers* series, and newsletters.

In addition to our publications, we organise four or five lectures during the year, the annual A.L. Morton Memorial Lecture, and occasional conferences on specific subjects. There is an admission charge of £1.50 for all lectures. The **SHS** also organises and sponsors joint events and publications with other sympathetic groups.

Back numbers of many of our publications are available and a list of them can be supplied on request to Mike Squires, 50 Elmfield Road, Balham, London SW17 8AL. mikesquires@btopenworld.com

The annual subscription to the Society is:
UK full rate	£20
UK concessionary rate	£14
Overseas full rate	£25
Overseas concessionary rate	£19

Subscriptions are due on 1 January each year.
Membership from January entitles you to copies of the journal *Socialist History* as they are published, and a copy of each *Occasional Paper* published by the Society, as well as *Newsletters* on the work of the committee.

Members joining the **Society** between September and the end of the year receive the second journal of the year and their membership will continue for the whole of the following year. All members enjoy the same rights to elect and to be elected to the Committee and the Society's offices.

You can join the **Socialist History Society** via the website (www.socialisthistorysociety.co.uk); by paying your subscription at one of our meetings; or by sending your name and address together with a sterling cheque or a postal order to: The Secretary, SHS, 50 Elmfield Road, Balham, London SW17 8AL